The Logistics Legends

Unveiling the stories of global influencers

Inspiring Journey from Adversity to Achievement

Behind the Scenes: Triumphs, Trials, **and** *Transformations* **of Logistics** *Titans.*

Published by
Signature Global Network PTY LTD

Copyright Disclaimer

© 2024 Cuilan Guo and Signature Global Network PTY LTD. All rights reserved. This book, including all intellectual property rights therein, is solely owned by Cuilan Guo and Signature Global Network PTY LTD. No part of this book may be reproduced, distributed, or transmitted in any form or by any means, including photocopying, recording, or other electronic or mechanical methods, without the prior written permission of the publisher, except in the case of brief quotations for review, commentary, or other non-commercial purposes as allowed by law. Unauthorized use is strictly prohibited.

Accuracy Disclaimer

While every effort has been made to ensure the accuracy and completeness of the information in this book, the author and publisher make no representations or warranties, express or implied, about the accuracy, completeness, suitability, or availability of the content. Readers are advised to independently verify any information and consult with professionals where appropriate. The author and publisher disclaim any responsibility for errors, omissions, or any losses, damages, or disruptions arising from reliance on this book.

Similarity Disclaimer

This book is a non-fiction work and includes real-life experiences. However, names and details may have been altered to respect privacy and confidentiality, and any resemblance to persons, businesses, or incidents is coincidental unless otherwise noted with explicit consent.

Opinion Disclaimer

The views, thoughts, and opinions expressed in this book belong solely to the authors and are not necessarily reflective of any affiliated organizations or entities. These opinions are based on personal experience and interpretation, and readers are encouraged to form their own views.

Explicit Content Disclaimer

This book may contain explicit language, sensitive content, or themes of a mature nature. Reader discretion is advised. The content is intended for an adult audience.

Expertise Disclaimer

While the authors have extensive expertise and experience in the fields discussed, this book is not intended to provide professional advice. It is meant for informational and educational purposes only. Readers should seek professional counsel for advice specific to their situation.

Ownership & Acknowledgment

While the co-authors have contributed to the creation of this book through their life stories and insights, all rights, ownership, and control over this work remain solely with Cuilan Guo and Signature Global Network PTY LTD. Co-authors have no claim to ownership or control of the content or intellectual property, beyond what is acknowledged here.

Publisher: Signature Global Network PTY LTD

Authors: Kristy (Cuilan) Guo, Rudee Bertie, Mandy Deakin-Snell, Ashwin Didwania, Gilbert Ernest, Derek Scarbrough, Deepanker Parashar, and Dr. Sri Rasamanickam

Cover Design: Kristy Guo & Signature Global Network Creative Team

ISBN 978-0-6456617-2-9 (paperback)
ISBN: 978-0-6456617-8-1 (E-book)

Content

Acknowledgments vii
Foremost ix

Chapter 1   Kristy Guo 1
Chapter 2   Rudee Bertie 20
Chapter 3   Mandy Deakin-Snell 103
Chapter 4   Ashwin Didwania 133
Chapter 5   Gilbert Ernest 144
Chapter 6   Derek Scarbrough 163
Chapter 7   Deepanker Parashar 193
Chapter 8   Dr. Sri Rasamanickam 210

Let's Connect 225
Resources 229

"Writing a book is not just an act of self-expression — it's the creation of a legacy that transcends time, a bridge connecting your wisdom with future generations, leaving a mark long after your voice has quieted."

Kristy Guo

Acknowledgments

First and foremost, to my amazing husband Luke, whose unwavering support has been the cornerstone of this journey. Thank you for managing our two wonderful children, Sze Sze and Selena, while I poured my heart into writing and editing. Your love, patience, and understanding have allowed me to chase my dreams. To my beautiful children, your hugs, kisses, and constant joy gave me strength when the work felt hard, and for that, I am forever grateful.

To my incredible co-authors, thank you for believing in this vision and for your trust in turning an idea into reality. This book is a testament to our shared passion and persistence.

A heartfelt thank you to my dedicated staff at SGN, whose hard work and commitment are the backbone of everything I do. You've been a constant source of inspiration and motivation.

To my coaching clients in the C-Suites, your faith in me pushes me to grow and succeed every day. I am honoured by your trust and your desire to see me reach even greater heights.

To my church community, your prayers and encouragement have been a guiding light, providing me with strength, balance, and purpose throughout this journey.

Lastly, to all the friends and supporters who have been there behind the scenes, your encouragement and belief in me have meant the world. This book wouldn't have been possible without each of you.

With deep gratitude,
Kristy Guo

Foremost

The baby girl's story

About 38 years ago, there was a baby girl born in a small town. She was not supposed to be born as it was forbidden to have the second child to be born during the year of 1986.

Background of that: in 1979, the Chinese government introduced a policy requiring couples from China's ethnic Han majority to limit themselves to one child. The official start of implementation came in 1980, with an open letter issued by the Central Committee of the Communist Party of China. The letter outlined the population pressure on the country and set out a goal of curbing population growth, bringing the nation's total below 1.2 billion at the end of the 20th century. As reports from the time noted, the nation's 38 million Communist Party members were told to use "patient and painstaking persuasion" to teach the rest of the population how important it was to practice family planning.

Source from times.com China's One-Child Policy: How It Started in the First Place | TIME

That girl fell from the house all the way from the 2nd story rolling down from the stairs, and miraculously survived.

That girl then suffered lots of health issues such as coughing for 3-4 months, getting the skin illness for no reason, and when she cries, according to her mum, she could almost be short for breath and always dying, which did save her a favour, for her mum said to her: 'Do you know why your father can hit anyone but never touches you?' The girl said: 'No, I don't know, why?' Her mum: 'Because every time when you cried, you almost fainted, your father was scared that you would die.' What a joke, but it's a true story! This girl did get an exceptional situation, but her childhood life was still a huge struggle. Why?

Her father was raised by the time that all sons were more important than daughters, and sons were supposed to be served and taken care of any needs they demanded. That was ridiculous, but that was why her father ended up doing anything he wanted. His life was filled with selfish needs, it's all about him and all about having fun in life.

Her father Wei didn't get married until his age around 33 which was very late in that generation. Back then, people got married and even gave birth at age of 17. 18. The whole reason why he's married is because his mum the girl's grandma who insisted and found a beautiful woman whose name is Zhen, and that is the girl's mum.

Zhen is the eldest daughter of 6 siblings. She's always the yes girl. She had no character, she had no desire, she is obedient, she is good-looking, but she's 10 years younger than Wei. The marriage had been a huge struggle since then.

They got married, had the first daughter and within less than 1 year, they had the other daughter and that's the baby girl.

The baby girl is me. That's the background story of my parents.

So, in short, I always joked to my friends who said to me how could you were born when you have an elder sister but the year of your birth you shouldn't exist? I would laugh and say: "I was the illegal one." Which was also why my mum had to get my ID later so that I would be safe. I believe they ended up paying some money to secure my birth certificate of showing that I am a legal kid.

My childhood was a miracle as I was left home more like an orphan even though I got to live with my parents who ended up going out to work at the factory from dawn to night. I had to learn how to survive and thrive all by myself.

When people look at me today, they would never have thought of any bad stories in my life. When they saw my positivity and achievement, they simply consider this as GOOD LUCK. I always believed that I would be the lucky one, which I guess it did give me more affirmation and confidence.

The darkest time in my life

Back to my parents' story, my dad's parents raised my sister because my parents couldn't handle two children at the same time. I felt sad for my sister, but my own life seemed dark every day. My dad was always coming home drunk, going out to gamble, and dancing at the bar, often not returning home until midnight or some nights not coming home at all. On the days he did come home, we were all scared, pretending to stay calm. He would come in, turn on the TV, follow his own routine, make noise, and act as if we didn't exist.

I love my dad, to be honest, very much. But whenever I think back on these memories, I become emotional, and my heart aches, filled with sorrow and sympathy for my mother. My father's lifestyle was never something I wanted for myself.

That's not the worst, the worst was the domestic violence. Every time when he came home, he started to shout, scream, scold mum, blame her. Countless times I saw dad hitting mum, pushing her, and many times when I wasn't there, the worst happened too. Once when I was studying abroad at my 13yo, I got a phone call from my grandma, who said to me: "My darling Grand Daughter, need your help!" I said: "What's up, Nainai (Grandma), are you ok?" She said with a crying voice: "Please persuade your mum to forgive your dad and get back to him. He hit her again and this time, it was serious, she ended up going to the hospital." I was shocked and I could not resist with my tears and then I said: "What? Why, again... ... Why is that happening." Grandma: "Listen my darling Four Four (my nick name), your mum only listens to you, you need to persuade her. OK? Promise me, OK?" I was too young to understand what's the right thing, so I did what she said. I called mum.

At the other side of the phone, my mum is crying: "my darling Four Four, he went too far this time. He hit my head, and my brain was badly inquired, and it might be a forever damage…… "I cried more, and my heart was ache, I was wordless but then I remembered that I needed to save their marriage, so I asked her: "Mum, do you still love Dad?" She paused for a while and then said: "I do, but what he does is too much, I am scared that I am going to lose my life." Me: "Mum, I love you…... and I am so sorry to hear what happened to you (boohoo)" Then I said: "Mum, if you still love him, and if he is willing to say sorry and truly apologize as well as guarantee no next time, then will you forgive him? If not, then you do not need to, ok? "Mum nodded, and as what Grandma said, she did listen to me, as grandma ended up persuading my dad to apologize to mum and so she forgave my dad once again. I didn't know if that was a good thing, or a mistake.

Throughout those painful time, I also suffered lots of health issues, and I blew up to be fat as it seemed to bring some joy to life is to eat delicious food. There was the specific period that my confidence level dropped down dramatically, and I started trying to hide away from people as possible.

Mum had nowhere to tell her pain, and so from the very early days, she encountered her belief in Buddha. She would keep asking for peace, day and night. She would take me to the temple and seek for her inner peace.

I cried a lot when I saw mum suffering. I was too young to understand what's going on in the adult's world. I was confused about what

LOVE and FAMILY mean as if my parents love each other and build up this family, why is their life so miserable and why was I feeling so sad for them both?

That made me want to escape and run, I started dreaming, daydreaming, night dreaming. I started writing journals, writing down my dreams, I started to comfort myself and kept myself strong. Outwards, I always had to pretend to be ok, so I was always the one faced all situations with a big smile. It's not because I was too positive, it's simply because when there's no light, I had no way to go, and I had to make a decision to be the light. Imagine a dark room, it does not need much light to be seen and instead of looking for lights, I was always the one who tried to be the light among all people and community.

My confidence was not very strong due to the broken family stories, but they said FAKE it until you MAKE it and I did make it. When I started to ignore the problems and focus more on the solutions and things I could do, my life seemed to be much better despite what happened to me.

Chase my dreams

I went further and further from home to study, to work and chase my dreams, but I would never forget to call my family, send them support. My first month salary which I remember it was only RMB 1500 in Shenzhen, it is around USD300. It allows me to pay my rent and for the rest, I sent home to my parents, and I had been doing that for more than 15 years and even until now I have always been willing to be one of their main supporters.

From moving to Changsha 5 hours by train far away from home at my age of 13 to moving to Shenzhen which is 10+ hours away from my home to work and live at my age of 17, to moving to Hong Kong at my age of 22 and then to moving to Melbourne Australia and starting from zero by abandoning everything behind. I was never scared of uncertainty, and I held huge faith.

Why am I sharing with you, my stories? The reason why I shared all of these with you is because I know that each and every one of us has stories, and in fact, many stories. Unfortunately, we all prefer to hide or not talk about it if we can. With the background of growing up, with the blaming and pressure from people around you, including our parents, we seem all tend to be reminded not to show our emotions, and not to express ourselves. Wearing a mask and pretending seems to make us safer and more powerful. At least those were my thoughts and mindsets for years! Not until… …

My authorship journey started

My journey of authorship started back on 15th September 2021 when the book I participated as co-author that was published globally. Little did I realized that I thought the life of others would be transformed reading my story, in fact, my life started an enormous change itself.

17 years of working in the logistics industry and my last role was finally bounced back to as high as before, reporting to the director and got chance to communicate with CEO directly. Most of my career I was dealing with C-Suites externally or internally. I had always been thinking like a CEO, working like a CEO and assisting all CEOs, but finally the voice hit me. The inner voice was saying to me: "Hey, you always want to share your story, and you have so many to tell. Why not become an author?" My burning desire drove me to every single step, and I took the courage and started my authoring journey.

At the beginning, I thought it's just an authoring and writing journey, later on I realized that it's indeed a healing and self-discovery journey as well. I started to look back at my life and I started to become more and more courageous than ever before. The more I share, the more confident and courageous I become. I realized that most of the time, it is not the situation or the environment that are restricting us, it is our own thoughts and yes, our biggest enemy is ourselves.

My friend, why am I so passionate about this? Because after so many years of knowing people from everywhere in the world. With more than 20K connections whom I met throughout conferences or in business and life, I realized that all of us are so different yet so similar. We are all humans!

Writing is the best thing for self-discovery and life reviewing. It is the best thing to know and understand who you truly are and who you desire to be.

Why running business and creating networks?

Are you familiar with the moment when you go to a networking conference, you felt awkward, lost and throughout the conference, everyone keeps asking you for business, business and business. All they care is YOU, NOT, it is YOUR BUSINESS.

What's worse, after the whole conference, it seems you talked to so many people but at the end you leave the conference, and no takeaway and people just come and go in your life? It is frustrating, right?

Hey, I've been in the logistics industry for two decades and being in leadership role for longer than that. After travelling around the world and attended countless conferences and in fact I travelled up to 15 countries and more than 30 cities before I was even 27. In meeting so many people, I understand how you felt!

I got it when there's hunger to grow business, most of us would want to directly go to the business part. We forget about the importance of keeping our faith in people and in networking. A true networking is to connect deeper to a human and building up a reliable and trustworthy long-term partnership. It is never about money. Unfortunately, 90% or almost everything in this world is running its way as the business and commercial way.

Which is why I started SGN a dream network to go different ways to build up a caring and strong united community that takes care of industry leaders while they are taking care of their business and people. Don't get me wrong, I am not perfect either and sometimes I could be distracted or pressed by the sales and revenue to run the company, which is why to keep a clear vision is essential, and to have a clear value guide and rule is significant.

If you are not familiar with whom I am now yet, I am the founder, CEO and President of SGN Signature Global Network, other than that, I am also an author, here are two of the books I have published, and I am a speaker, coach and I coach high performing C-Suites who own 7 figures and working toward to their 8 and 9 figures too.

I have been supporting C-Suites to achieve their huge life and business goals, and I have witnessed so much success for people and their breakthroughs after they joined our network, business wise and personal wise.

My biggest passions are dreams, faith, purpose, leadership, effective communication and personal development.

As you heard from my childhood stories, in my life, I suffered from pains and challenges, while it's so dark that I had to stay positive and optimistic all the time. Like many of you, I assume that when my mind got stuck, and when I felt I was not loved and unworthy, there's even the thought coming to my mind to finish my life. I'm glad I didn't. When the pain was too much, there's only one way to reduce the pain, and that is pretending it's not pain, it is joy. That's exactly what I was doing throughout all these years.

To reflect the other side of me while going through those hard times, I decided to be the light when there seemed to be no light. I decided to make people laugh so that I could forget about the pain in me. I decided to lift others and build up families in the communities wherever I went. I decided to give people around me and to appreciate people around me so that they wouldn't feel how my mum felt and how I felt. I decided to bring hope to people and be generous to people, always be courageous to point out the great thing about that person, which had helped me to win huge influence and impact wherever I went.

In the year 2014 when I got my sponsorship from the company in Melbourne, Australia one of my dreams coming true, I submitted my resignation to a company where I contributed my youth with for 10 years and to say goodbye to all the achievements, my fame, positions and great income. It's the courage and determination for me to do so, and I had no idea what's in front of me, but I knew there's always hope and surprise.

To my surprise, my ex-boss didn't give me garden leave, they trusted me that much and they gave me three months to hand over my work to at least 4 senior managers. The last day of mine, I got the M.D. and whole management crew going with me for a huge party to farewell me. A few days later, when I informed my classmates in Uni crew about my departure, they all came to farewell me. Even up a few months ago, when I said I would go to visit in China for a bit, that I did not expect any gatherings. All those CEO classmates and friends from so far away, drove a few hours to see me and to meet me, and they still respect me as the leader of them from 20 years ago. One of the classmates who used to be a class captain said to me another day on the phone: "Kristy, do you know? You are always so unique and special; you are always courageous, and you just create followers automatically." I said:" Thank you." She then said: "Do you know one thing I would never forget. You are the only one who got 100% votes by the class for your election in class."

I didn't remember this, but WOW, I am so happy to hear that. Honestly, I'd never been thinking of this at all, as all I was doing is to serve, to help others, and to make a difference. I created so much great memories to the class and school, and the reason why I am confident is not because of my past, my childhood or my parents' stories, not even my appearance as I had been the chubby one and was struggling with my shape. It's the Ds, **d**reams I had, **d**ecisions I made, the **d**edication I committed, and the **d**etermination that then drives me to be whom I am today.

If I can do this, so can you! If I made it, so can you!

How the co-authoring starts for the logistics legends

In my life, many impossible things turned from ideas to dreams and then to realities. This book is one of the ideas that is now the reality. It cannot be here without the initial idea and dream, and it cannot be here without the commitment from the other amazing author contributors and impossible to shine its value without your support and reading it.

It is a privilege to co-author this book with so many wonderful souls. Trust me, people who participate in this book are those visionaries, who dare to dream and to take an action, who commit to what they say and who are fearlessly marching forward despite of setbacks, doubts and uncertainty, they are the real deals.

It's not an easy journey to find all the committed people like the current co-authors, and believe or not, the only reason why this world is falling shorter of trust is because that so many people give broken promises or over-promise things then they didn't delivery. This is completely out of respect to everyone, unfortunately this is the reality which I found out the main reason is not that they want to break any promises, if simply because they doubted themselves, they doubted their own decisions, they doubted if they could make this happen, they doubted that if the time would be enough to make it happen, and they doubted that they would be distracted by the journey of writing when they needed to fulfil other duties, or they simply could not see the beauty of sharing their stories and leaving a legacy. I remember a famous saying I learned when I was little: When you make a decision, go for it, don't doubt, keep going and never give up, and you will always succeed! Some other sayings like: Great people don't do the right things; they make everything right.

The key is not about finding a place where everyone is living and safe, but to keep breaking our comfort zone to explore the best of life and to live a life that is not just about ourselves, but a life with more meaning and purpose!

I was shocked that even though many top leaders, and successful people who appeared to be successful but inside of them, they are not feeling secured or good enough. They have huge doubts about themselves, which is crazy.

The truth is, my friend, anyone can do it! All you need is your passion, purpose and your faith.

What are these stories to do with you? Because I believe that these stories will inspire you to re-awake your dream, re-firm your faith and re-find your purpose, re-strengthen your leadership and effective communication skills and transform your personal growth.

The Logistics Legends

Why logistics? Why logistics legends?

First, even though the book's name is the Logistics Legends, but it is not restricted to be the Logistics Industry at all, in fact, it is resonated to everyone in the world.

Despite we are in the logistics industry, logistics people are overall super resilient.

Logistics plays a crucial role in the global economy, and its importance is underscored by several compelling facts and data points:

Economic Impact: The global logistics market was valued at $9.96

trillion in 2022 and is projected to reach $18.23 trillion by 2032, growing at a CAGR of 6.3%. *Resource from Logistics Market Size & Share Analysis | Forecast 2032 (expertmarketresearch.com)

Job Creation: The logistics sector is a significant employer worldwide, providing jobs for millions of people across various roles, from truck drivers and warehouse workers to supply chain managers.

Trade Facilitation: Efficient logistics can increase trade by 15% or more when a low-income country improves its logistics performance to the average level of a middle-income country. *Resource from Connectivity, Logistics & Trade Facilitation: Development news, research, data | World Bank

Cost Influence: Logistics costs have a greater impact on trade costs than tariff barriers in most countries. Improving logistics performance can be more effective in promoting trade than reducing tariffs.

Global Supply Chains: The ability to move goods quickly, reliably, and at low cost is essential for coordinating global production chains. Poor logistics infrastructure is a major reason companies avoid expanding their procurement networks to emerging and developing countries.

Trade Delays: A one-day delay at the border leads to an average 1% decrease in trade, highlighting the critical role of efficient logistics in international commerce.*Resource from Customs Delays: The Waiting Game: How Customs Delays Act as Non Tariff Trade Barriers – FasterCapital

Technology Adoption: The logistics industry is rapidly adopting new technologies. For instance, the global logistics automation market size is expected to reach $121.3 billion by 2027, growing at a CAGR of 11.5% from 2020 to 2027. Resource from Global Logistics Automation Market to Reach $121.27 Billion by 2027 (prnewswire.com)

Environmental Impact: Logistics plays a crucial role in environmental sustainability. Embracing sustainable logistics practices can lead to long-term cost savings by reducing fuel consumption, energy use, and waste disposal expenses.

E-commerce Growth: The rise of e-commerce has significantly increased the demand for efficient logistics. Global e-commerce sales are projected to reach $6.3 trillion by 2024, driving the need for more sophisticated logistics solutions. Resource from Global Ecommerce Sales Growth Report (2024) – Shopify

Crisis Response: The COVID-19 pandemic highlighted the critical role of logistics in global crisis management. Logistics providers were essential in distributing medical supplies, vaccines, and maintaining supply chains for essential goods.

These facts demonstrate that logistics leaders are pivotal in shaping global trade, economic growth, and sustainability efforts. Their decisions and innovations have far-reaching impacts on businesses, consumers, and the environment. As the world becomes increasingly interconnected, the role of logistics leaders in optimizing supply chains, adopting new technologies, and driving sustainable practices becomes even more crucial for global economic development and environmental stewardship.

The Logistics Legends Short Overview

This book is filled with legendary stories from ordinary people from UK, USA, Australia, Mauricius, India, Sri Lanka, Netherlands, Switzerland that have achieved extraordinary things in life.

When you are reading, my friend, I am sure you can apply each one of them to resonate with you. The message we have here is that you can be whoever you believe you can! Working in one industry doesn't mean that you are only valuable in that industry. We as humans, have huge potential that we are surprised how significant they are!

For my story, I am sharing not because I am recognized as the legend myself, but more to prove to you that our life is not fixed unless our mind is fixed. Owning a growth mindset and being courageous to restart from zero any time and anywhere equips me to do what I do. To walk the narrow path where not many people, dare to walk.

I am not that special, as I said at the beginning. If I am special, so are you. You will be amazed by all these stories behind the scenes where everyone can only see the ice burg, not what's underneath.

I am blown away by all these authors hearts, their dedications, their determinations and their driven force, you will be surprised by the similarities they have despite the vast difference they have; weather is their gender, age, background or culture.

Throughout reading all these stories, remember to reflect all stories to your own life and I guarantee you that each and everyone's story is a mirror of yours. I encourage you to be empowered and inspired by them and gain your motivations again to face your life, and you would be so proud of yourself by reflecting your own journey.

I am not going to ruin the movie to tell you the ending when the movie hasn't even started yet, but I'd want to share a bit of things about these amazing authors here for you to get excited! Shhhh... ...

Remember: as humans, they are logistics legends, I am logistics legend, you are logistics legend, and we are all logistics legends!

Rudee, a highly respectful individual who owned three companies and has influenced thousands of people in his life. He would never say that to you as that's what I have observed. You would be touched by his thoughtful heart and beautiful soul. His love for his family, his authenticity and true heart dealing with people. I would always call him The Thought Leader. He's not just a successful person, but a humble person and his authenticity inspires thousands of leaders and followers in his life.

"Rudee, the hoody!" His story takes you through a history and his life throwback overview. Rudee is an amazing storyteller, and you will enjoy his story so much.

Mandy, a fearless female leader who has so much courage to fight for what she desired, and her legendary story never fades by her age. She's strong but humble; she's tough but willing. Her story can inspire you so much, and I do not want to disclose to you here, so read and find out yourself.

Ashwin, his story shocked me, and if you are looking for any excuses not to do something, after reading his story, you have no way to find excuses not to achieve things. His determination, his resilience, man… … Not because of his legendary story itself, but also his huge influence received countless recognitions globally. His story is a living example for mission impossible.

From an ordinary person to become a pilot? Move to a new place and learn a new language at the older age? Find out from his chapter!

Gilbert, not just because he is an entrepreneur and a part-time but professional singer. His positive mindset and resilient spirit have led him to triumph in both business and personal challenges, making him a respected figure in the logistics and entertainment industries.

Gilbert's story could empower thousands of leaders and young people who are struggling or in the middle of the mist. Read his story will empower you to solve your problem and stay positive all day.

Derek, his fearless spirit to share his bold story touched thousands and if his story does not inspire or touch you, nothing will.

Every time when I read his story, I become emotional. He is not just a great storyteller, but a living example to show the world that your past does not define you. Trust me, when you start reading his story, you won't want to stop.

Deepanker, a humble and the nicest guy who cherishes relationships and his way of dealing with people soften your heart and enables anyone to work with him.

His story reflected so many from India and indeed reflected many Asian countries. All of us may see ourselves in part of his story, so go dive in and find out yourself.

Dr Sri, his journey had so many turning points and if he would have made a different choice, he wouldn't be where he is today. Winning people's heart, re-starting from a new journey, being courageous to make tough decisions, these all made him who he is today.

His chapter is written fairly short, but it tells a life story of him. He may not be very talkative, but his action and achievement set him apart from many. Read his story and you will have your takeaway.

Before you dive into the incredible stories ahead, remember that each one is more than just a tale of success—it's a gift. These stories are filled with hard-earned wisdom, raw resilience, and powerful lessons, wrapped in the lives of those who have dared to rise above.

Every author in this book has navigated through challenges, embraced change, and shaped their legacy in the logistics world, their world and the world. Their stories are not only an inspiration but a roadmap for you to discover your own potential.

As you turn these pages, think of them as keys—unlocking new ways to lead, to dream, and to overcome. Each chapter is a beacon, showing that no matter where you start, greatness is within reach.

The Logistics Legends

You'll feel the courage of those who have gone before you, and you'll be reminded that you, too, have the strength to carve out your path.

Let these stories fuel your spirit, guide your steps, and remind you that in this vast world, we are all legends in the making!

Best Regards,
Kristy Guo

Chapter 1

Kristy Guo

My story

Fast forward back to my childhood

My given name is Cuilan. I was born in a small town in the central south of China, and it is called Shao yang. If you don't know where it belongs to, it is in Hunan province where the current first lady in China of year 2024 was from.

Loving arts, performing, singing, dancing and drawing. Throughout my childhood, every day is about creating. Didn't end up choosing the art school, due to the humble situation of my family. We rarely had enough to survive. Mum and dad were just workers in a chemical factory. That is why I chose to go to an early university to study my major which I always had been passionate about – English. I believed that to learn better English could then bring me better opportunities to earn incomes for my family.

My early University life

Throughout the university, with the limited RMB150 (around USD30) per month to survive, I often could afford buying things I like, which wasn't pleasant as a teenager. My teenager years seem to skip away as all I got was responsibilities and understandings. I had to survive from being far away from my families and I had a mission to complete which was to learn quickly the skills then I could start to be financially independent and support my family.

Looking back, it's the best experience with limited materials, which had shaped me a person who never really chases materials, instead, I had to put my joy in learning and connecting with people instead. I graduated from university when I was only 17 years old which was usually the normal kid's year 9 age.

I left home at my age of 13ish to study in the university which is far away from my family, and it was in the other city, and I studied there for around 4 years. Throughout this time, I was trained to be a resilient and stronger girl who learned to be happier, better despite of tears.

However, I do remember vividly the day when my dad sent me and drop me off in the university and knowing that my coming few years will be living in one room shared by 6 people, zero privacy. The feeling was weird. After he left, my whole life was filled with uncertainty and mixed feelings. I was nervous yet excited, I was feeling weak yet stronger. I still remember that night after Dad left the gate of the school, watching his back image disappearing, finally I burst to tears for no reason. My individual journey completely started at my age of 14.

With a heavy heart, I went back to my dormitory and was surrounded by a group of strangers who were my roommates. The first night was full of gloomy mood and my colour was blue.

But the second day, I immediately became like a re-born child, who started to break my comfort zone and to know everyone in the room. No doubt that night, I ended up making all room mates doing cat walks with me. They laughed so bad and had the best time in their life. From that moment on, I knew I got a special gift. A gift to wake up the inner child of anyone, a gift to bring sunshine and joy to someone's life, and a gift to bring light when there's darkness.

Side note: Funny enough, the event I am running nowadays never get rid of the catwalk traditions. I remember the third morning, one of my roommates said: "You are unpredictable and amazing! The first night when you came, you were so quiet, and we all thought you were the quietest and shyest one, my goodness, you are the most active one!!" I laughed and the inner me knew that I am both. I was quiet for a long time and I was trying to give things to people around me, things I didn't get throughout my childhood but I get to build up for other people.

What did my Uni life do?

I always believe that everything happened for you, not to you.

My university life completely shaped me to be a more courageous and happier person. I wasn't wealthy in money, but I felt that I was the wealthiest person on the planet back then.

Why? First, I got to stay away from my parents' problem and drama and to have my own life connections and that distracted me so much from worrying them. Second, I got to participate every single program and to learn everything and try everything. From being the podcaster to news journalist to sing, dance and compete speech as well as debate. From learning Taekwondo to playing guitar; From playing ping pong ball (Table Tennis) to basketball; I am not afraid of failure and my life seemed being the BEST than ever. I was like a bird who just flied out from a cage and seeing the world.

Because I had the experience while my parents were away that I had to learn how to know people and break ice as well as making new friends, this skill of mine seemed working super well at school as well. I knew almost everyone, student, teacher and even the cleaner. I loved to connect with everyone, and I treated everyone with my whole heart, which then brought me the 'famous person' in the university. Everyone talked about me, everyone respected me. To them, I was just one of the most talented person as I was literally everywhere and whatever I did, I did well. Through attending lots of activities also made connecting with many new friends. They were my biggest supporters, and they gave me hope when I knew there's still inner family wounds inside of me that takes time to heal.

Life is funny sometimes, throughout my university time, I didn't need to read anything before or after classes but every time after the examination or test, I got to the top student. That impressed my teacher and my classmates too. I had so much fun organizing things in class and in school. Every day was a blast, which not just brought me more confidence but also so much wealth. My wealth? Joy, abundance, friendships, recognition, helping others, influencing others. I had been our teachers' best helpers and there's the time I ended up teaching our class to sing English songs. I simply learned those songs by listening to the radios and tapes. I was obsessed with learning new songs, and my singing skills were madly improved too. Throughout the school years, I went to competitions and always got high ranking. The fact I could be nominated by our classmates to teach them made me feel like the luckiest person in the world. My value was my wealth.

There's the darker side too. The darker side is the struggling with my limited monthly fee, and I did not want to call parents to ask for more. I was that kind of person who just wants to take all responsibility and let others feel good and less worried about me. Seeing many classmates and roommates buying new stuff, dressing like a princess, going out for shopping and buying things they like. I was just one of the companions and to save my face not to tell them that our family wasn't rich enough, I persuaded myself to believe that I was a princess and queen, and I was just different than others and I was more mature than many others. So, every time when they wanted to buy things and when I wanted too but could not afford it, I would just say things like:" Well, I've got something similar already, don't need more, no need to waste money." It's very hard for a girl of 14 to say and to resist but I did it most of the time. There was still the time when I really loved one outfit, and I had to save for two months then went back to buy. But the way how I changed my thinking made me feel great and the family condition and the limited money didn't define me to be lower than anyone else, instead, it made me feel more confident than ever!

Secret story never revealed before – Turning point for the future

After graduation, within less than 3 days, my career started officially and forever. I found a job in a small freight forwarding company. To me, man, what was that? As a graduate, it does not matter to me what it is, all I wanted was to find a great work environment and get started. So, I accepted my job which I only did the interview for once. I remember it was 8th March the International Women's Day, what a great time to memorize. I was officially financially independent. The journey there was short, it's only around 6 months. Little did I tell many people about this missing part. The company I worked with had huge amounts of money and every day they ate like a royal family. The boss drove the most expensive car...... to me these were all normal. Not until one day my brother-in-law saw the company sent me home with Benz and he asked me the question: "Isn't suspicious?" I said: "I don't know... ..." But right after that day, the company hosted a team bonding gathering to the Karaoke.

I was very mindful, and I never allowed going alone to any place I didn't feel safe, so I asked my friend Lisa to go with me. Lisa's one of my besties from university, and she agreed.

When we arrived there, everything seemed normal. The boss's nice and the other staff members were super excited. We entered to the Karaoke room, and this is a SPA place where you could also play games or table tennis. I love table tennis, and I didn't like the feeling of staying in a room with many men and strangers. I never go to bar in my life and despite my extrovert personality, I didn't really enjoy an unhealthy social life, particularly from what happened to my dad when I was little, I was more against that. I had my standard, so Lisa and I sneaked out to play table tennis instead.

However, after around 30 minutes, when we went back to the room. Lisa stopped me before I was about to open the door. She said: "Wait, shhhh" with a face full of suspiciousness, she said: "Look, what are they doing?" My mind was blowing… … I had zero idea what that was, but it does look familiar. Just like what we saw on those movies when people are taking drugs. They put all those white and crystal-clear power stuff. I had no idea what they were. But they started being crazily dancing and completely lost themselves. I covered my mouth, full of awe, fear and uncertainty. I needed to make a decision fast, so I grabbed Lisa's hand and say: "Let's run… … "I wanted a pure life and a wonderful future. We so we ran away and then figured out a beautiful excuse to say to the boss that we had to leave due to some emergencies.

Long story short, I resigned from that company and started to search for a new place. The company kept looking for me and trying to persuade me to go back and I would never. The thing is, when you were young, you might not know what you wanted exactly, but the core values of ethics must be clear. I am so glad looking back that I had a clear vision of my future life. I didn't know exactly how it would turn out to be, but I knew exactly what I shouldn't do. A great reminder to any teenager and young adult.

What if I wasn't courageous enough to change? Many years later, that company was gone. The suspiciousness wasn't coming from nowhere. I am so glad that I did, or my life would have turn out to be so different. Your courage to make hard decisions matters!

My dream chasing journey

The first dream coming true was to participate the TV show with my sister. She was 20 and I was 19. Back then the trend is to have a DUO and partner as a vocal sister band. We sang and danced together, and we were chosen to be the final.

It was a great experience yet many ups and downs. 7 days in the hotel with another 23 candidates. 14 girls and 14 boys. The show was called I act, I show in Shenzhen TV.

So many of us dreamed to be a superstar when we were little and when we saw those superstars on the stage, so did I. But I didn't just dream, I am a doer. I was not afraid of trying until I found the way. Prior to that, I attended auditions from different channels, and I was selected by one of the star agencies to call them, but I didn't. I still wanted to be responsible for my job. The Job I got from HLS Group where I helped achieving huge success afterwards. The job that built me up and shaped me to be whom I am today.

Coming back to this dream experience, I was on the stage, I got my classmates and colleagues being my supporters and fans. How awesome was that! But for me, I was more grateful than feeling like the top of the world. It was that experience completely killed my dream to be a superstar! If it wasn't that, I would have still been thinking to be into the entertainment industry and be the actress and singer. Remember when I was little, I was very good at singing, and I even won the awards in university as well as teaching my classmates to sing? Sometimes, you never try, you never know.

Why am I not interested in that anymore? Because there's too much dark truth behind the scenes.

Other dream footsteps were mentioned on my previous books The Joyful Leader In You and The Joyful Balance Code. Long story short, the other big dreams I had achieved were:

1. Travelled around the world up to 15 countries 30 cities before my age of 27.
2. Got the job sponsorship from Hong Kong and moved to Hong Kong from Shenzhen.
3. Got the job sponsorship from Melbourne and moved from Hong Kong to Melbourne, Australia, started a new life in Australia.
4. Wrote my book and became the international author with best-selling books.
5. Started my own network and coaching business.

There are more... ...

My corporate and networking journey

My childhood experience shaped me to be a courageous and outgoing person who can talk to strangers in less than 1 second and get to know them in no time. I remember vividly once I went to travel to Sao Paolo with our President Vincent and two other colleagues who were also taking care of Latin American trade. It's a breakfast time while Vincent saw a guy who also wearing the delegate lanyard for the Intermodal event. He said:" Kristy, can you go and get his contact?" Me, with no second thought, within less than 1 second "Sure!" immediately went up to say hi to that guy and after 3 minutes, we had a great chat and I got his name cards and gave him mine and understood immediately his background and potential areas we could cooperate with.

When I came back to Vincent and my colleagues, Vincent smiled with pride and said to my colleagues: "Told you, learn from her, team!" Then I realized that it was a test, and my two colleagues clapped their hands filled with admiration. Little did I realize that my passion for people trained me to be a people and networking person.

I love people and I love to spend time with people, particularly from different nationalities.

The company I worked with which was called HLS a freight forwarder who just started its overseas development internationally while they were only doing domestic business when I joined them. Fitting to the best time, I was the first one creating my own department and I helped to translate all Chinese cards to English. I created my own department and increased the department to 26 people while assisting the company winning thousands of overseas partners and equals to millions up to billions of businesses which they call it nomination cargo. Funny enough, 90% were nomination cargo which was built up by me and my team together with the President and Vice President. The M.D., on the other hand, was focused on dealing with local service providers relationships. The company had grown from 50 people to 4000 throughout my time there. Amazing, right?

One thing I was prouder was the value I brought wherever I went. Through the 10 years working in HLS, I had become the right hand for the three shareholders as I put all my heart, energy and time serving them and worked as if it's my own company, every single day. Sometimes when they had argument or issues, once it went through me, they immediately become happier and came to an agreement.

My youngest time from age 17 to 27 was spent in that company. Beautiful memories, beautiful feedback and the day I left bringing my team to the KTV to do farewell for me paid by the M.D. who said to me: "Kristy, I don't know how you did that, your team is super united, and you have a special and unique way of leadership style and skill."

I didn't just meet the overseas partners, but every time I would write down the meeting minutes and follow up all details no matter how late that night was. I would never procrastinate, and that habit has still been helping me to become who I am today.

After meeting those networking partners, I memorized each of them with something special and unique about each person and mirroring their personalities to make friends with them. We are all humans; this is not a rock science. I would always spend time to follow up with each one of them and ensure they are taken care of until the job is done and closed. HLS thrives and grows significantly throughout the 10 years I was there. Ranking top 5 from far east to transpacific lanes. My way of business development Department has become the lead to all freight forwarders particularly in China. We lead the trend.

Lessons I learned

They say you would learn more from failures than from success. Here are something I learned:

Never be able to compete with my appearance or family background, I focused a lot on my person development and bringing value wherever I went. From being leader all the way through my university period to being the stage manager, director, playwright, producer, costume designer, house designer, light designer, sound designer, actress, makeup artist…… From being the chubby one and got a nickname of little piggy to become one of the most popular people in the university across all grades and genders. How do I know? Because even now the teacher who taught me still wanted to connect with me and told me all of these, and every time when I needed to go back to China, a whole bunch of old classmates without my request would just appear, even though they were busy running their own business or they needed to drive 3 hours. I started to realize that wow, man, I had created huge invisible wealth!!!

Be clear about your core values and stick to them. Throughout all these years, I had faced huge trials and temptations whether it is for name, fame or money, but I always stayed in my holy zone. My childhood life gave me too much pain, I would never want to make any bad choices in life. It doesn't mean I would never make mistakes, I will, and I did. But the core value guided me and will guide me to the right direction whenever I need to make a tough decision. Dignity, reputation, pure heart, kindness, humility, these are the things we should always keep within us. Trust me, they have guided me until now and that's when I can laugh loud, smile authentically, as nothing can stop me to be me and to be the changemaker to make this world a better place!

My secret weapons?

1. Bringing joy and sunshine to people.
2. Seeing the best in everyone and lifting others.
3. Focus on my personal growth, don't wish my life is better, wish I am better and stronger.
4. Do everything with your 100% commitment and treat people with a true heart no matter how they look. Time will tell and you will be rewarded by that habit.

Lessons to success? (2A + 2B + 2C + 2D)

Action

Action speaks louder than words, only actions can kill your anxiety. Overthinking will kill your confidence and delay your success. The biggest failure in life is only thinking not acting.

The truth is, if you act, even if it's wrong, you immediately can tick away one unworkable way and get closer to the victory.

My whole life is filled with action. How did I turn all my ideas and dreams to reality? Action!!

Attitude

Without a good attitude, it is impossible to succeed. Without a great attitude, it is impossible to find joy in life.

I am always filled with an attitude that I can learn from anyone in life. Being a sponge, opening hearts to listen and learn. Take advice not orders. I still need to filter the things I have heard.

Trust me, I made lots of mistakes by listening to many people and sometimes taking too much advice, which is why I have become more sensitive and firmer than ever when hearing advice. Again, advice is good, listen and think, but we do not always have to take the orders. We are the leaders of our own life.

Belief

Without believing, it is impossible to succeed. So many of us stopped chasing dreams or bigger goals is not because we are not capable enough to do so. It is simply because of our limited belief.

It took me so long to understand about the true meaning of the sky is your limit. If you can dream of it, you can achieve it!

My friend, time for you to check what are the false beliefs you have that have stopped you to become better, stronger, and bigger? Don't shrink! Because trust me, there are always people who are waiting for you to shrink so that they will feel better! Don't live a life for them!

Your life is short, live it fully! Live an extraordinary life and believe in yourself, never give up!!

Boldness

It took me very long to be willing to be a public figure and share everything online and writing my book too. I didn't understand the power until I realized that it is like a wound you have from the past, the more you try to hide it, the worse it will become; But as long as you are willing to remove the mask, to embrace the real you, the true you. You will fall in love with yourself more. I am not talking about self-obsession, it's the basic love that we need to have for ourselves.

My boldness of sharing my weakness and stories helped me to be much stronger.

My boldness of holding the truth helps me to attract the right people into my life. People come; people go. True friends will stay!

The key is since my focus is no longer myself, I have nothing to fear about. My boldness can help to bring hope and future to others!

Courage

Courage is the big topic particularly for a female and a girl who was born in a little town in China. I thank everyday to my courage. My courage to dream, to do, to lead, to make a difference!

If it's not because of my courage, how could I be coaching world-class C-Suites who are even 20-30 years older than me? If it's not because of my courage, how could I be willing to throw all my old achievement from HLS days with both money and power, and started from zero in a new country? If it's not because of my courage, how could I gather the busiest people in the world to write this book?

My friend, my story is a living proof to you that anything is possible!

Be courageous to be who you are! Be courageous to chase your dreams! Be courageous to start from ZERO every day! You will see surprise unfolding in your life every single day.

Commitment

Why are there the same group of people with the same age, background, IQ, EQ but the outcome is different?

Poor people have 24 hours, and rich people also have 24 hours. What makes them different?

Mindsets, yes, but one more thing which is the flavour that cannot be separated from making the soup of success, and it is your commitment.

When you are 100% committed and responsible for your results, trust me, you can always achieve huge results!

I had been dealing with successful CEOs who were already quite successful but all in a sudden, their business seemed to be slower. We found out it's his commitment, and right after we agreed with the commitment he made, his business immediately got rocket high peaking up. The biggest month he had increased up to 400%. How crazy!

Desire

Just like the commitment, if your desire is not strong enough and if your goal is not clear enough, you will slow down for no reason.

Imagine you are walking at the forest without any purpose, what will you do? Hanging around, doing nothing or random things. Just like a day without a plan, you will be led by your day; instead, if you plan your day, your day will be led by you.

Desire is an interesting thing. If you look back, when you had a huge desire, you will always find way to achieve that thing. Nothing could stop you from getting it. Just like a hungry person who hasn't had food for 4 days, you do not need to feed him, he would grab the food himself and look for all ways to get the food.

Often when we are falling behind or losing motivation is because we haven't found out our true desire, the true why behind it and the clear destination where we are heading to.

Hunger is the best gift for a person to be more successful than anyone!

Discipline

No matter how much you do or say, even if you read all the fancy books, went to all top seminars and workshops, after acting, it is about the discipline to keep us on track.

We are all animals of habits, if a habit is not built up yet, it's very likely to be broken shortly.

I once said to my followers: "The highest form of freedom is discipline." Isn't that true?

I can write books and keep talking to you, but if I am not even doing the right thing myself and self-disciplined enough, will you still listen to me? No!

I have been doing morning exercise in the last 3 years, almost not missing any day except for on the air travelling. I still do if I am at the hotel.

I have not been watching TV for at least the last 8-10 years and always spending time reading, listening audiobooks, learning new things and writing.

If I cannot do it myself, how can I coach my clients and my people? If I didn't have the high self-discipline, it is impossible to get what we have today.

Success is just the iceberg surface; it is the disciplines with sacrifice that helped to shape whom I am today.

Thank you for reading my story and I'd love to hear yours!

I am excited for my future, as being the speaker, award-winning business and life coach, I am recently recognized by the New York Time as the The Fearless Force Behind World-Class Success & Global Leaders. I am grateful. I know my dream to empower 100 million global leaders and to make a huge impact on the future leaders is still a bit far, but it is possible! My dream is that one day when we wake up, the world is as one. There's no bias, only understanding, compassion and love. You may not be aware how powerful one person can be!

Don't believe me? The history told us itself:
Mahatma Gandhi's Nonviolent Resistance (India, 20th century)
Gandhi led India's independence movement using nonviolence, inspiring millions. His philosophy of peaceful protest helped end British rule and influenced civil rights movements worldwide.
Source: Britannica

Rosa Parks Sparks Civil Rights Movement (USA, 1955)
Rosa Parks' refusal to give up her bus seat to a white man ignited the Montgomery Bus Boycott. Her quiet act of defiance became a catalyst for the broader U.S. civil rights movement.
Source: History.com

Malala Yousafzai's Fight for Education (Pakistan, 21st century)
After being shot by the Taliban for advocating girls' education, Malala Yousafzai became a global symbol of resistance. She went on to become the youngest-ever Nobel laureate.
Source: Malala Fund

Nelson Mandela's Leadership (South Africa, 20th century)
Mandela's fight against apartheid, despite 27 years in prison, led to the dismantling of racial segregation and his election as South Africa's first Black president.
Source: BBC

Marie Curie's Scientific Breakthroughs (Poland/France, 19th-20th century)

Marie Curie's discoveries in radioactivity changed modern science, making her the first woman to win a Nobel Prize, and the only person to win in two scientific fields.
Source: Nobel Prize

If they can, so can you, and if I can, so can you!
The dream will be hard to fulfill without you!
Join me to this changemaker journey!

Now, get excited to read all those legendary stories!!

Kristy Guo
The Visionary Behind C-Suite Transformation

Kristy Guo is a **dynamic leader** in global logistics and an **award-winning business and life coach**, recognized by *Forbes* as a **multicultural networking expert**. Hailed by *The New York Times* as "**The Fearless Force Behind World-Class Success & Global Leaders**," Kristy has over **two decades of experience** guiding C-suite executives to achieve **unparalleled success** while maintaining a **balanced and fulfilling personal life**.

As the founder of **Signature Global Network PTY, Signature Growth Academy**, and **The Joyful Leader in You** brand, Kristy has **carved a unique space** for herself as a **premier coach and speaker**, helping logistics industry leaders **optimize their business strategies** and **life goals**. Her **multicultural background**, combining her **Chinese roots** with her **Australian identity**, enables her to offer a **holistic approach** to **global leadership** and **business networking**.

Kristy is also a **prolific author**, having published **three books**—one of which is a **co-authored program**. Her other two books, **The

Joyful Leader in You and **The Joyful Balance Code**, have both achieved **best-selling status on Amazon**. Her works, focusing on **leadership** and **personal development**, have earned **widespread recognition** for their **transformative impact** on readers.

Her **career accomplishments** extend far beyond publishing. Kristy has been **instrumental** in helping organizations **build thousands of international business partnerships**, resulting in **billions of dollars** in business growth. Known as the **"C-Suite Whisperer"**, Kristy's ability to empower executives to **thrive professionally** without sacrificing personal well-being has made her a **sought-after coach** in the global logistics sector.

Her journey is not limited to the corporate world. As a **best-selling author, award-winning coach, speaker, influencer, and dedicated philanthropist**, Kristy embodies the **balance** she teaches. Her **mission** is to empower **100 million high-performing C-suite leaders** to **amplify their income and impact, expand their influence**, and create **lasting global change**. She serves as a mentor to **world-class leaders** and is a **beacon of hope** for future leaders, **breaking biases of age, gender, and culture**.

Off-stage, Kristy enjoys life as a **devoted wife** to her husband Luke and **mother** to their daughters, Sze Sze and Selena. She actively participates in her **local church** and dedicates time to **charitable work**, firmly believing that "**in lifting others, we rise.**"

Kristy Guo's **visionary leadership, holistic approach**, and **relentless commitment to excellence** make her a **catalyst for global transformation** in both **business and life.**

Reach out to Kristy: linkedin.com/in/cuilan-kristy-guo-1776b5182

Chapter 2

Rudee Bertie

The book

From what I remember: what I know.

My earliest recollection as a child growing up; I remember me, my mum and my 2 sister Jacqui & Linda, Caren wasn't born at the time, sitting in the back of a taxi coming down ledgers road on our way home from our grandfathers house on the hill side. We lived in Chalvey Grove at the time, a house shared with my father's sister, Rosie, her husband Boom and their 2 children, Clive and Julie, our cousins.

I'll come back to talking about growing up in Chalvey Grove later because I want to finish off telling you about the story in the taxi coming down ledgers road.

I whispered "mummy, he's got a gun", I was probably barely 4 years old at the time and I saw this metal object that appeared to look like a gun. "Mummy the man had a gun" my mum sushed me up as to say, keep quiet and don't be so silly. I couldn't believe how calm she was because as far as I was concerned, if you have a gun, you must be the bad guy and you're going to shoot someone. With that I said it louder, I couldn't let it rest, I said "mummy" this time the man who was actually the driver turned around, I said; "mummy – he's got a gun" and with that, the man reached for the metal object, pressed a button and a light came on. The man smiled and said "it's a torch silly, look." My mother and my sisters laughed, and so did the driver as he continued to drop us at home.

I remember the first house we lived in was 190 Chalvey Grove, Chalvey, Slough, a house my mother and father shared with his sister auntie Rosie and her husband uncle Boon, their 2 children Clive and Julie my cousins. So, 2 families, 3 bedrooms, 1 house. We shared the bathroom and kitchen, and I think the front bedroom was for my auntie and uncle along with the living room downstairs at the front of the house and me, my 2 sisters and my parents had the two rooms upstairs at the back of the house. I think I have that right, that's how I remember it anyway.

I remember being in that house from birth until I was 4 years old until my mother registered for a council house and we moved out of the old and into the new must be around 1972 into 136 Spackmans way, Chalvey, Slough where I lived for the rest of my life up until I was about 19, 20 or 21. The dates right now are blurred because, even though I moved out of the family home when me and my sister Linda bought a flat together for £29k – in a building called SaltHill mansions, very posh, located on the bath road / three tuns, Slough, we spent a lot of time back at the family house, especially on Sunday for Sunday dinners.

Now let's get back to how it started for me.
Born in September 1968 in Taplow (Canadian Redcross Hospital) Buckinghamshire, England.

My mum called Francis even though that wasn't even her real

name and my dad Rudi, short for Rudolph, eventually after 3 children moved into their own 3-bedroom town house where my 2 sisters (Caren wasn't born yet) shared a room and I had my own bedroom. My sisters' room was at the back of the house over the garden and overlooking the other neighbours back yard whereas my bedroom was at the front of the house, next to my parents' room, overlooking the road that came into the estate alongside the green playing fields across the road adjacent to the motorway. I could see the motorway from my bedroom window and for as long as I could remember I gazed out of the window every moment I could get as soon as I woke up in the morning often wondering where all those people were travelling to driving their cars and Lorry's very fast up and down that motorway. My dad used to always tell us if we ever got lost, remember we live off junction 6 of the M4 motorway. The M4 ran from east to west of the country, from London to south Wales with Junction 6 being Slough central 10-15 minutes' drive from Chiswick junction 1. Later on in life when I passed my driving test and bought my first car, a metallic green ford escort mark 2, it felt like the right thing to do, get the boys together, jump on the motorway and drive all the way to Wales, spontaneously, with no experience of motorway driving, no fear, no care in the world, where going to a different country and we'll be there in a few hours.

From my window, I would always see airplanes flying over the house and the motorway, we were on the flight path, not too far away from Heathrow airport so I would think maybe the traffic was going to the airport and people were travelling to far and distant places or simply going to Windsor castle to see the Queen. Windsor castle was on the other side of the motorway in the distance, and I knew when the Queen was at home because I could see the flag flying, blowing in the wind from the castle tower, that is what I was told anyway.

I used to think, when I got older, where was the first country I was going to visit. At first It was America because we used to watch American tv like Starsky and Hutch, The streets of San Francisco, lieutenant kojack, Colombo, happy days, Dallas, man from Atlantis and king fu, you get the drift, lots of action packed cops and robbers usually, still to this day I prefer these type of movies but then over the years, as a became a student of Karate, learning how to count from 1 to 10 and some basic Japanese JP dojo etiquette, had me curious of the far east, especially Japan, so this surely must be the first country I would visit and explore especially now, I had a clear sign that Tokyo Japan would be the destination, not only because the master karate instructors came from there and if you wanted to be the best you had to train with the best but one day I opened up a magazine and this sticker fell out with a photo of Mount Fuji.

The image was as clear as day, I stuck it to my wardrobe door so that I could see the image every day when I woke up to when I went to bed at night. I believe in seeing is making it happen. It's always been my way. Display an image of something you want to achieve, put that image somewhere you can see it always, it will remind you to work towards your goals and not take it down until you achieve what you set out to do. Guess what, to date, I've never been to Japan, that said image is imprinted in my mind, I will be there one day, it will happen.

It was a nice house with some very nice neighbours, so nice that most of our block or the two blocks on our stretch of the road are still in contact to this day, obviously not everybody, but we do what we do to stay connected, could be Facebook or a WhatsApp group or just simply through the grapevine. 3 bedrooms, bathroom on the top floor, the middle floor you had the kitchen and the living room, we called it the sitting room then down stairs was the garage, the meter room another toilet and the washroom/ the laundry room that lead into the back garden where my dad would grow vegetables mainly potatoes, tomatoes, onions, lettuce, cabbage, carrots, peas and thyme, probably more provisions but this is what I remember, also strawberries and blackberries but no other fruits at least I don't think so anyway.

As kids, we all played together as neighbours, in and out of each other's houses, doors on latch, always welcome and your parents would always know where to find you. On weekends and during school holidays, we could leave the house in the morning and wouldn't be seen until the evening, but parents knew that us kids were always safe. Either at one of our friends usually playing some kind of creative game or simply chilling, scheming on what adventure to do next.

A multicultural neighbourhood/ like the United Nations, most of the time we all got along. Racism existed but on our street with our crew, in our community on that estate, when you saw it, you dealt with it and when you dealt with it, you knew it was real. As kids, we interacted with each other, discriminating against each other wasn't a thing when all us kids were in single figures, but as children get older and ages move into double figures, the changes appear through the cracks. Learnt behaviour is on display, in your face, very loud, very vocal and obvious. You get to understand that people are different, you don't want to be around certain people, naturally we form different friendship groups, I suppose that's called growing up.

At the age of 4 I started infant school, we called it infant, some call it primary school, not because I was a smart genius of a kid but more because when my mum registered my older sister Linda to start in September, Linda is a year older than me, less one week, so not actually a year older, she took me a long, obviously my other older sister Jacqui was at school, she's 3 years older, my dad was a work, so I couldn't stay home by myself, so I went along with my mum and my sister.

The head teacher Mrs. Northern asked my mum why she wasn't registering me at the same time, me and my sister look alike, we were probably the same size because apparently, I was a big baby and my sister was a little premature baby, we could pass as twins. My mum used to dress us in matching clothes but in different colours, boys and girls typical colours and no I didn't wear a dress or a skirt. Mrs. Northern obviously thought we were the same age and when my mum explained I was a year younger and would only be ready for school next September, Mrs northern said don't be so silly, and insisted that I join school the same time as my sister and that was that. This is probably why we have such a close bond even until today and still share some of the same friends as well.

Of course, this arrangement suited my mum because it meant she could go back to work and have some time to herself while us kids were now all at school. I'm sure she wanted a bit more time to herself, but knowing my mum the way I do, she probably took this as an opportunity to get back to working days rather than the night shift she used to do. I always remember my parents juggling around us, so I imagine this to be the case.

I've always liked school, I've always liked the social aspect of school, the educational side was okay, but I much preferred mingling with the people. Even at that early age, I always felt that there was more to life than going to school, getting an education, finding a job, paying bills and being content and happy with what you have.

The paper round (my first job) (from papers to trainers)

I remember it like yesterday, the sun newspaper was advertising a racing bike at a cut price for something king like £49.00, I needed a bike, I wanted to have that one because in my teenage years, I didn't have a bike, I was expected to ride the same bike that I had when I was about 10'years old, plus now I was working on my paper round, I knew that a bike would be more efficient than walking and I would probably be able to take on more papers and deliver them quicker on 2 wheels rather than on foot.

When I first started my paper round, I wasn't earning very much, was about £2.50 per week then rose to £2.75 per week. Big bucks/ big money when you are only 11 years old. I remember my first day, first week on the job, it snowed every day, and it was freezing. I wasn't even prepared for the weather conductions, I had a little bomber jacket that I inherited from my uncle Johnny, it was blue with white and red stripes and was the warmest jacket I owned. With no gloves on my hands and nothing fancy on my feet, my fingers and toes froze as soon as I left my house until getting back later in the morning before school. Did I tell you the whole reason why I started the paper round in the first place, I wanted a pair of trainers, they cost £12.49, was all the rage and everyone was rocking adidas kick or better, I just wanted adidas kick, black with white stripes.

I went to my father and asked for a pair of adidas kick, he said, well, if I have to buy you these pair of expensive trainers, your sisters are going to want the same, I can't afford it. I said please dad and at which he said, let me see. Now to me, 'let me see' usually meant NO, so with that, I figured I would make my own money and buy my own trainers and would ask my parents again for nothing because I knew the answer would Always be NO.

My good friend Adrian, fondly known to us as Rhino, told me that his brother was doing a paper round and that the newsagents were looking for other paper boys, so I went along for the interview, had to get permission from my parents because I was only 11 and started immediately, like the next day.

Doing that paper round taught me a few values, for example, be disciplined, work for what you want, earn it and you will get it. So, I saved my first wages for my first pair of adidas kick. I went back to the shop "Guilloids" I think that was the name on the Windsor Road opposite the rising sun.

I went in full of confidence, armed with cash and ready to use it to buy my first pair of trainers. "Hello," I said, I was here to buy a pair of Adidas Kick size 8. The shop assistant went to the back and came out with a box—wow, Adidas Kick—wow, size 8—wow. Now, bearing in mind I'd been to that shop before, so I knew the price and the size I wanted, but when the assistant came back and asked if I wanted to try them on and I said no, I just wanted to pay for them, he said, "Well, young man, that will be £12.99." I said I don't have that, as last week they were £12.49, and I don't have enough. We agreed that they would hold them for me until I came back with the right amount of money. Literally, in a couple of days, true to their word, they held the pair for when I came back. But when I went back into the shop, I looked around again for a bit, then realised that I liked the Mamba, Bamba, and Samba instead and decided to save some more to purchase my first pair of Samba for £14.99 instead.

Having the ability to earn your own money and buy things without asking your parents was the best, most empowering feeling at that time. The formula was simple: work, earn, save, spend—easy, right? The formula never changes; only the stakes get higher. Work harder, earn more, save more, spend less... literally, that's what I did, and it felt good being in control. It was the first time I felt that I could control the outcome—being able to see something, wanting it, and having the ability to have it and take ownership of it. To me, that was powerful and felt good. I did that paper round for around 2-3 years until I became a teenager, 13 or 14, when I picked up another paper round from the same shop, first thing in the morning before school and way before people went to work.

Two paper rounds soon became three, and three became four—yes, all before school and yes, way before people left home for work. How did I achieve this, you may ask? Good question. Well, following my method of work, earn, save, and spend, I purchased a bike to help me out. Being an early riser anyway, still the same today, I would be up by at least 5 a.m., quick wash, get dressed, and out the door before sunrise. I'd cycle to the shop, pick up the first two rounds, deliver everything in the sack quick time, then back to the shop to collect the other two rounds that were nearer to home. I'd complete the deliveries quick time while logistically figuring out the most efficient and convenient route with enough time to spare to get home, change into my school uniform, chill for a bit, and then head to school.

School started at 08:55, or was it 09:05? I don't actually remember the precise time; it was either 5 to or 5 past the hour—that's what I remember. But more importantly, I was never late and always on time. Where we lived, as the crow flies, the school was probably less than 5 minutes away. As most people are not crows and couldn't fly, the route along the road would probably take you 15 to 20 minutes at a good walking pace, so you would be safe to leave the house no later than 08:30 hrs to guarantee being in school on time and ready for registration.

My sister Linda would always leave the house way before I did but was always late or only just getting to school in the nick of time. Whereas on the other hand, I would leave 5 minutes before the bell rang and always got to school on time, in time for registration, with never a late or absent marked against my name. Using logic, logistically, my good friends, still to this day, worked out that if we took the shortcut alongside the rubbish dump, through the allotment, we could easily shave 15 minutes off the time to get to school. So, Carty (Kevin) and Richie (Christopher) would knock on my door as they had to pass my house to get to school. Normally, I was in no rush, so they would come in, sit down, and chill for a bit before leaving for school. Normally, walking at an easy pace, getting halfway down the road, we would suddenly hear the school bell ring. Then we would start running as the crow flies, alongside the dump, cut through the allotments, through the compost heap, climbing over the fence or squeezing through the hole in the broken part, across the field, past the swimming pool that was more like an ice skating rink in the winter, through the side door, and straight into registration class—always in time to say, "Yes, sir."

My name would always be called in the top three, alphabetical order: after Baines and Bartrem, it was Bertie.

Although I was always involved in a lot of after-school activities, being on the football team, basketball team, athletics team, and cross-country team for about 2 weeks (the 2 weeks only referring to cross-country), I was capable of long-distance running, but I didn't like it too much, so I dropped it quickly. I remember one time I was picked to be on the team, so I went along with the rest of the group to compete against other schools in the district. I was quite fit and knew I had enough stamina to compete, so obviously, I went out to win the race.

Having never done this before, I knew no better and pushed hard, put my head down, and ran at a good pace from the start. Before I knew it, I was way ahead, in front on my own, with a pack of 3 or 4 other boys behind me. I could see a crowd of people, teachers, and bystanders in the distance encouraging me on. What? I'm in front, about to win the race. This is easy!!

Anyway, I got to where I thought the finish line was, and I heard the coach say, "Great run, Bertie, now keep your pace and go around the circuit again." I didn't know, or I wasn't paying attention, but nobody said twice! Wow. Immediately, my legs started to slow down, I was out of breath and feeling the pressure. One by one, everyone else started to pass me. So, from being in a strong position, leading the pack at the front, I slipped into 2nd, 3rd, 4th position, hung on for a while, then in another instance, I dropped all the way back to 10th position and still had a fair way to go. This was the moment I knew I messed up, and definitely the moment I knew cross-country wasn't for me... ha-ha.

A couple of days later, I was picked again for the team to race in the district. Apparently, the coach thought I showed good form and had ambition but just needed a little more coaching. I tried everything to get out of that race—all the excuses under the sun. The coach, our head sports teacher, Mr. Moore, had none of it and said the team needed me. "We have a good chance to qualify for the county meetings if a few of us get in under the qualifying time," he said. I told him I didn't want to do it, and with that, he said, "You have to, otherwise you'll be letting down the rest of the team."

I said, "I was only on the team for a week, and I didn't enjoy cross-country and didn't want to take part." He insisted that I had to do it, but me being me, I decided otherwise. I said, "You should take someone else who really wants to race. I'm not doing it." He said, "Yes, you are. I'm picking you. You're on the team." I had other ideas and decided to take that race day off sick from school, just so I didn't have to compete in the bloody cross-country race that I had no interest in.

Anyway, to cut a long story short, the team performed well in that race; they qualified for the county, so they really didn't need me at all. The next morning in the school assembly, Mr. Moore made an announcement to the whole school that the cross-country team performed well, but one person let us down. Everyone knew who that one person was—well, everyone in the cross-country team anyway. He continued, "If Rudolph Bertie wasn't ill yesterday, we probably would have been district champions, but we wish him a speedy recovery and get well soon." I thought, "You bastard. What an axxxhole! From that day on, I never liked him, and he never liked me. We didn't see eye to eye. He showed me no respect, so I gave him none. Regardless of him being the teacher, basically the boss, the man in charge—you can't force respect, you have to earn it. He wanted to bully me into doing something that I didn't want to do, and I simply said no.

The king of clean. (2nd job)

My after-school activities never stopped me from taking on another job after school.

I registered with a temp agency (temporary work agency) as I now had the bug, work, earn, save, spend. I think this was my calling, I was born to work, I was born to steer my destiny in the right direction. In order to achieve everything, I set out to do, I knew I had to put the time and the effort in. I was very active back then, in and out of school. The agency sent me to work in an office in Windsor cleaning offices. This was a big step up for me as I would be earning big bucks. I think it was something like £5.50 per hour, 2 hours cleaning for 2 to 3 evenings a week, I'm going to be rich I thought, so off I went to earn a bit more.

It was easy work, easy to get there as well even though I was too young to drive and didn't have a car. The agency would arrange to pick you up, drop you to the office then arrange to collect you from the office and drop you back to the pickup Spot. Easy, just don't be late and you'll make money, I thought, I was never late, even if I had a school football or basketball match, I was never late, always on time.

I suppose I did the temporary contracting for a few months until the supervisor Alice asked me if I wanted a permanent cleaning job, every evening, within walking distance from where I lived, for 2 hours, start at 5:30pm and finish at 7:30pm and get paid £17.50 per week. "Of course," I said "sure" to me it was a no brainer. I already thought the work was easy, I actually enjoyed cleaning, still so today, it was normal in my house, it was how we were brought up. You dirty something, you clean it, you move it, you put it back, basics, simply makes easy.

At this point I thought I wouldn't mind working in an office, I had no clue doing what, but I just thought it was a nice safe clean environment to want to work in.

I was allocated the 3rd floor, to clean all the offices, desks, dustbins, vacuum the office floor etc.; then clean the hallway where the lifts (elevator) and stairs met. I especially liked seeing my reflection in the chrome elevator doors and liked to use the buffing machine that polished the tiled floor as to me it was a bit more exciting, and I felt like it was a skilled job. I worked fast, I moved very quickly around the 3rd floor, but I would spend a bit more time in the toilet is giving the toilet, urinal and the sink that little More attention to detail. Toilets must be clean, right? I had no issue scrubbing and wiping in those contaminated areas, it was my job to clean and I wanted to do it to my best ability and be the best at what I do.

Supervisor Alice approached me again and said, "Rudolph, me and you need to talk." I thought, oh shit, what have I done? She said, "The company asked me who cleans the 3rd floor, and I asked them, 'What has he done, what's happened?' They said quite the opposite." What they said to Alice was that the person who cleans the 3rd floor should get a raise because they do it very well with a lot of attention to detail.

Now that made my day! I definitely felt respected that people would appreciate the work I was doing even without knowing who I was. I felt good—over the moon, to be exact. Alice continued to say, "Rudolph, I'm giving you a pay rise to £19.00 a week, but I also want to give you another floor to work on because you work so fast on the 3rd floor and always have time to spare. You might as well do the 7th floor, finish within the same time (2 hours), and get another £19.00 per week."

Well, you can imagine—life simply couldn't be better! £38.00 a week, plus my paper rounds; I was swimming in money, felt like I was in heaven already. Alice really looked out for me. She knew my parents from around the way, but I didn't know that, and at the same time, she didn't know I was their son. But we clicked. I liked her, she trusted me, and I trusted and respected her, still to this day. She calls me one of her sons. I never let her down, and she always looked out for me, which I loved her for.

The trust Alice put in me didn't stop there. She was also the supervisor at the local Tesco supermarket under the Queensmare in the high street. There was a temporary cleaning job for an hour every weekday morning. I was still doing my paper rounds, still going to school, still doing all my after-school activities, and still cleaning the 3rd and 7th floors in the ICL (International Computers Limited) offices at the top of the high street. In a nutshell, I was making it work. I was a very busy, busy bee—fully active, earning my own money, saving at the same time, and now in a position to be able to help my parents at home financially.

Not that they wanted to take money from me because I was still a student trying to make my way, but my little contributions helped a bit here and there, I'm sure.

Leaving school in the mid 80's (going into the real world) (Mr. Bean)

Fast forward to 1984, the year I left school at 16 years old without a clue in the world and did not know what I wanted to be or what I wanted to do, probably normal for most kids my age at that time. Even though I didn't fail my final exams, by no means did I pass with flying colours or anything like that. The careers officer was useless. His name was Mr. Saunders, he drove a mini, nothing wrong with driving a mini but he was like 6 foot 6 tall all squashed up knee to chin in this mini, he looked like Mr. Bean, exactly the same way Rowan Atkinson played the character. If I didn't know any better, I would think that Mr. Bean character was based on Mr. Saunders.

He was useless, he said I should be a labourer, a brick layer on a building site, start at the bottom and work my way into construction, get a trade he said. Nothing against builders, but it wasn't for me, I told him so, not for me, doesn't appeal to me. That was all the advice he had, go to the building site, get a job. There was no discussion of further education in college or university, not that I was looking down that path anyway but at least have the conversation with me and give some kind of encouragement, but nah, nothing like that. I felt at this stage in life at that particular point, I was on my own. Don't get me wrong, my parents cared about everything, but they weren't pushing me down any road. The rule was, if you're not going to college or university, you need to get a job. It was clear what needed to be done but what. What was I going to do with the rest of my life? Having the conversation with my father, he advised me never to work outside and never work in a factory. I thought that's rich coming from him because since arriving from the Caribbean, he did both. He was advising me based on his own experience. As a child you see your parents go to work, but you don't think anything more about it, you never knew whether they loved the job or hated the job, more times than none, they hated the job but liked the people they worked with. Eventually it's all about the people. He didn't want me to experience what he had to go through so that was his advice.

Somethings are meant to be.

I really didn't know what to do in life, but I knew I wanted to work, I didn't want college or university, I just wanted to work, I was used to earning by now and wanted to take my earning potential to the next level and make a career but in what, I didn't know.

I heard there were apprenticeship openings for electrical installers at British Telecommunication (British Telecom) now known as BT at the nearby Langley college. I was told I'd have to have an interview and sit an exam and have a colour blind test. So off I went to Langley college one morning and when I got there the hall was already packed with school leavers my age queuing up to sit the test. Wow I thought, how many apprentices are they going to take on? There must have been at least 200 people in that hall so good luck to anyone that got accepted. I was quite chilled about the whole thing, but I liked the sound of being an electrical installer, everyone needs electricians right, that was my approach.

They eventually got around to me, I say the test wasn't that hard, based around math and common sense really, advanced to the interview and I felt like the job was mine already. Sailing through the interview, I think they liked me, then went off to take the colour blind test, which to my surprise I failed. What?! How could I fail a colour-blind test, I'm not colourblind, a little short sighted, but definitely not colourblind.

This was the test; was similar to a flick chart, a set of numbers and letters in various colours, some of the text was typed normally while others where in dotted figures, written in different colours at different angles with some letters and numbers over lapping, put together on what I could only describe as A4 size type book. They would flick the pages, so everything looked like animated images, and you had to say what you saw. Apparently, I was seeing something totally different to what was actually there, so I suppose based on a lack of clarity, I failed the test. Devastated I was at the time because I thought I surely had the job and it was an job that I found attractive, it had something about it that warmed me plus it wasn't factory work and it was inside work to start with.

Anyway as I got my head around what just happened and come to terms with what to do next, I was walking towards home, through the high street, I contemplated doing a little bit of temporary work with a friend of mine who picked up a delivery contract with Wicks; they sold (homeware/garden furniture / decorating/building) goods, which I ended up doing for a short time a few weeks before which took us all over the south of England delivery goods and even at times setting up some of the furniture for the customers. That was quite interesting, but it was very short term only, I would say a week or so when, as I was crossing Windsor Road, looked up and saw a big sign above a two story office building that read "THORN EMI DATASOLVE" and in brackets said, learn new office skills and be placed in a career within 6 weeks after some training.

That sign changed my life forever, but I didn't know it at the time. Some things are meant to happen. This got my attention as I was intrigued as to what they did inside. I wanted to understand what office skills they would teach, was it an office like the ones I was cleaning at ICL or something new, something different. It couldn't hurt to have a look but I was still skeptical because in my eyes office work wasn't manly work, I always saw it as a career path for women, as this is all you saw on TV but I was intrigued so I walked up the small flight of stairs to the entrance went inside only to be greeting by a really nice lady asking me if I came in for an interview. I said I didn't come for an interview, but the sign caught my eye, and I was wondering what it was all about and more importantly interested in understanding how to get on the career path after 6 weeks.

She went on to explain that there would be a course on basic office skills from typing with a type writer and computer, word processing, photocopying, operating the facsimile (fax) machine and telex machine, things that I've never done before and it interested me even more because when I was still at school, we had a science and physics teacher called Mr. Sloman, he said that computers will never take off and that they would never work but I argued with him at the time to insist that technology would take over the world and we needed to keep pace with new technology or get left behind. He thought I was just being disruptive and didn't have a clue what I was talking about, but you tell me Mr Sloman, who's right and who's wrong now? Anyway, the lady asked if I wanted to have a look around, I nodded in acknowledgment, and she pointed and said: "after you as we proceeded down the corridor into another more vibrant room."

Wow was the first thing that came to mind as I saw at least 20 people, all kids my age, doing exactly what the lady had referred to earlier, getting on with things and learning office skills. I was impressed. I was even more impressed when I turned a corner into another room and walked straight into my next-door neighbour, Mark Napper, not only did we live next door to each other, but we were friends to, still to this day, he was a year older than I was, but we always hung out together as kids from the early ages of 5/6 year olds. He said, "what you are doing here boy, have you signed up?", I laughed and said "NO" but I will now knowing that you are here. I made a joke and said something like "I didn't know you like doing women's work" he replied and laughed and said "guess who else likes doing women's work? look over there, look, Scott Paul, Winston Lake and Martin Daniels" we both laughed, I was like wow, if it's good for them it has to be good for me too.

We all chatted for a while and the guys were encouraging me to sign up immediately and learn some new skills as they had been there for a few weeks already and some of them already had a placement to go to after the 6 weeks training. I haven't told you about the best part yet, they would also pay you to learn new skills, cover your lunch and travel expenses that came to £27.50 per week/ £110.00 per month. They also helped and guided you to open up a bank account, not a saving account, but a current account, and taught us how to manage our finances and how to pay our wages into the bank. Back in those days, we got paid every week with a pay slip with cash in a little brown envelope. They wanted us to manage our earnings without spending our hard-earned money immediately and wasting it on things we didn't need. I was doing this for a few years now because I already had a bank account at the local TSB but that was a savings account but the current account with the Lloyds bank, the bank of their choice, probably because it was down the road and easy to open up an account there without any credit history, having a current account was different to having a saving account, it was good guidance and a valuable education.

I started at THORN EMI DATASOLVE the very next week, I loved my time there, I felt blessed, learning new things very quickly and progressing fast. They found me a placement within 4 weeks at a firm called MEADOWS AIRFREIGHT which wasn't that close but wasn't that far nearby in Colnbrook right next to Heathrow Airport. Apparently, Meadows Airfreight derived from "Sir Thomas Meadows" probably the biggest freight forwarding/ removals company in the business at its time. They had offices and branches everywhere, but I had no idea what freight forwarding was, all very alien to me, apparently airfreight was a big thing, who would know, living near to the airport watching all those aircraft on the flight path for all these years growing up as a kid.

Finding my feet at Meadows Airfreight.

I was a fast learner and picked things up quick, life at Meadows Airfreight took me first into the accounts department working with Angela Evans, then very quickly Angela noticed that accounts wasn't for me and that I needed to do something a bit more creative and thought provoking rather than accounts where she could see that I was getting bored easily as I would be finishing all the set tasks very quickly. It was decided by the company that they would move me into the IMPORTS department and although I was no longer working for Angela, I would always see her in the canteen or would simply pop into her office for a chat, a cup of tea of coffee and sometimes I would take her in a flask of hot chocolate that I made every morning from home. Angela was cool, we got on well, but I think she liked my secret ingredient hot chocolate more.

Imports were for me, I knew it from the start, it felt as if it was made for me, and I took to it like a duck to water. I was learning new skills; I was carving out a new career path. I was still under the wings of THORN EMI DATASOLVE as a YTS trainee (Youth training scheme) something that the government set up with local businesses in order to teach kids my age new skills and trades, get us into work so that we were not unemployed, and the unemployment numbers looked good for the government as well. Lots of kids my age around that time 1986/87/88 would go into a YTS scheme and be taken on as full employees of that particular companies. The YTS was in every profession across the board, from office to banks to factory to sports and entertainment, football, the film industry, engineering, the police force and army, navy etc.; you name it, and it was there.

The YTS was a massive success for the government, at £25.00 per week minimum was a win-win for the government and the business alike. Meadows offered me a full-time contract in 1986 of a whacking £3,700.00 per annum, approx. £71.00 per week followed up very quickly with a pay increase to £4,600.00 per annum, approx. £88.00 per week to show their appreciation for my understanding of my tasks, hard work and dedication to my job. I was a fast, neat worker and would find other jobs to do outside of my job description and what they paid me to do. I needed to be busy and also felt like I was making a difference within my department. I was definitely the youngest in my department, made friends very quickly and always wanted to learn from everyone else around me.

At first, I used to get the bus to Colnbrook, but it wasn't direct from home so I had to walk to the bus station in slough central, catch the 81 bus to Hounslow and get off at the punch bowl and walk down for about 10 minutes to get to the office which was on the left hand side of Poyle Road just before the motorway crossing of the M25. The site today is a Travel Lodge hotel. Then I started to cycle to work.

It was good in the summer but in the winters was a different story, by now I was taking driving lessons, and I couldn't wait for the test date. As confident as ever, I knew I would pass the test and be able to buy a car to drive to work. In the meantime, a manager from another department, the import consolidation manager, a guy by the name of Mike Salmon lived near me and asked if I wanted to be picked up in the mornings and he would bring me to be with him in the mornings.

Mike was a good guy; he loved his cricket and would always sing songs on the way in. I think he loved his job because I don't think he missed a day from work in all the time I was there. He had a company car, he had a beige Ford Fiesta mark 2, the engine size was only 1.1 liters, but he drove that little thing as if he was racing formula one. I was grateful for the lift in the morning and sometimes after work as well, mostly he worked later than I did because he was the manager, or he wouldn't be going straight home from work so I would normally catch the bus back which was fine.

When I started my first paper round and delivering newspapers to those people's houses all those years ago, I would see nice cars parked up in the drive ways or on the streets outside the houses and would always wish one day that I would be owning one of those cars like a BMW or Mercedes or a SAAB because they were different to the normal British vehicles you would see on the roads. I especially could see myself driving a BMW with my jeans and hoodie, the way I dressed then and still the way I dress today when I'm relaxed and unwinding. I could see myself stepping in and out of that BMW and people asking me what I did for a living, and I would say I'm a businessman and leave it at that, have them guessing in speculation if I was somebody. Ha ha! Normally, you would only always see middle aged white men driving these types of vehicles, no-one else could really afford those cars because they were pricier than the average Ford or Vauxhall. Little did I know then to what I know now, these men were probably managers or sales executives or something like that and the combine they worked for probably suppled them with a company car.

One day I said to my boss, she was my supervisor, I said "Della, one day I'm going to have a company car, I like what Mike and you drive, I like the Fiesta!" She said: "not here you won't," in her slight London cockney accent followed by "people have to die in here before you get given a company car and look around everyone looks healthy around here so I don't think so" – we both laughed about it, she was that type of character, a very smart lady, sometimes serious, she wasn't that many years older than me but she was firm at time but had a jokingly manner about her. I liked her a lot and up until recently we spoke about those days, and I asked her if I was a little toe rag back then asking loads of questions and getting up to too much mischief and you know what, she said, no far from it, she thought I was a very decent young man with a big future ahead... bless you Della Whitworth.

Like I said earlier, I took on other jobs outside of my job description or created work outside of my remit. One of the jobs that I created and was responsible for and one that I was very proud of was creating a system for the filing room. I had my files in order, ship shape where they were easily found when filed away, I didn't like when others went into the room and messed up my system as it would create extra work for me. I like things simple and would rather do things myself rather than allowing others to do their own filing if you know what I mean? It wasn't even my job, but I soon got the title of chief filer or something like that, my files, my filing system, leave it alone.

My real job title was "import call outs" At the top of the room you had the import consol department, then you had us the call out department, where we would call the customer and advise the arrival of a consignment and take the clearance instructions then we would write up the files in preparation for the entry department where they would eventually complete a customs declaration and clear the goods through customs. Now this I was interested in, the customs clearance department, this intrigued me for the longest while, I wanted to be that person, I wanted to be the person that completed a customs entry declaration as I felt that was the heart and brain of the business especially working within the imports department. Helen Harden was the assistant manager of the import department and Jan Dupka was the import manager of the whole department. Because Jan didn't know me like Della and Helen, Jan thought I was lazy and didn't do anything, it wasn't because I was, you know I want, it's because I work fast and neat so whenever she came around it always looked like I wasn't doing anything. Helen and Della always used to tell me to slow down but I didn't listen, they obviously knew what was coming. I remember one time I was so bored because id finished all my work that I pierced a plastic cup from top to Botton with drawing pins, creating in my head what looked like piece of art. Jan walked by and went mental, she was pissed off either with me or with my supervisor for allowing me to be sitting at my desk do nothing but nonsense.

When I explained to her that I had finished my work and had nothing else to do, she said what about the filing, I said done, what about the write ups, I said done then she shouted at Helen, give this boy something to do, we are not paying him to be sitting around doing nothing. Yeah, I was in trouble, I used to think Jan was okay, a nice boss lady but for some reason, she didn't like me much, or that's what I thought anyway. Another time I recall, I worked with another guy called Paul, I don't remember his surname, but he was probably in his late 30's to mid-40's, he sat in the desk next to mine, he was in the middle, I was at the end and Mark Long sat at the other end by the window. Now in my eyes, Paul was the lazy one, always just doing enough, a proper typical nine to five, never late, never early, starts fidgeting at five minutes to five in the evening, tidying up his desk and smack bang on 5pm, out the door so quickly that you could see him driving out of the carpark approximately 2 minutes later. He would take 10-minute fag breaks on the hour every hour sometimes on the half hour in between tea and coffee breaks all day and for some reason that was acceptable, but I was the lazy one. One day I remember having a conversation with Jan about why I needed a pay rise because I was doing both my work and Paul's work.

Her words puzzled me at the time when I asked why Paul was getting paid more than I was when I was doing all the work. She said, well Paul is a married man with commitments, he has a family to feed, he's experienced and knowledgeable, that's why he gets the big bucks and you're just a trainee. I felt disrespected and didn't appreciate her remarks. Airfreight forwarding was a good career to be in, I knew it, I was learning everything insight apart from customs brokerage in the customs clearance department. I wanted to learn how to be a customs broker and asked several times to be taught how to do customs entries only to be met with answers like, it's a specialist job with lots of responsibility, takes years of training that comes with accountability, it's a difficult job and you must be diligent and accurate at all times as it comes with risk of consequence customs interrogation and penalty fines, you wouldn't like it and if you did, it's too much pressure you.

The guys that worked in that department didn't want anyone else to know how to do their job, because it was so specialist and everything else that I mentioned, for those guys, they would always be in demand, and it was a job for life. I especially remember a gentleman by the name of John Prynn. He wore a brown cardigan with a grey or green shirt on most days, brown, grey or blue trousers and always grey socks with brown sandals, yes, you heard me right. This guy was so good at his job, he was always in the office, he smoked like a chimney and lived in Colnbrook around the corner and would walk to work. He was always the person that was on call out and would get lots of overtime. He or any of the others didn't want a young buck like me learning their trade and competing for their jobs. I remember whenever I had to go into the customs brokers office, I would have to knock on the door and wait to be called in. It was like the secret service in there. A room full of smoke, I always imagined as I saw the cigarette smoke gush out of the door whenever opened, you would hear utopian musical instruments playing until the door was closed again.

I remember one time entering the room and everything stopped, everyone covered up their documents with their hands leaning forward until I left the room. As soon as I exited, everything started up again, wow! This was normal practice, very odd behaviour I thought, and I'm sure it would be detrimental to the business as a whole. Any business should want to teach the next generation and encourage the tools of trade for sustainability you would think – right? I felt it was time to move on, if I wanted to pursue my dream of becoming a customs broker and driving a company car, I would have to leave the good people behind at Meadows and continue my career path elsewhere.

Priority Airfreight. (game changing)

Back in those days, you could walk out of one job in the morning and into another one that same afternoon. That's precisely what happened on the day that I decided that I needed to move on from meadows to pastures new.

I saw the job advertised in Skyport, the local airport newspaper, and went for it the same day and got the job. At the interview I was supposed to meet Givvy Suman, the import manager, he was supposed to be taking the interview. As I walked in the office at lunch time, I could tell it was lunch time not because I went there in my lunch break but because the office was fairly empty and quiet and the odd person there weren't actually working but rather sitting, relaxing, eating sandwiches or something with a coke, Fanta or cups of tea or coffee on hand. I was greeted by a gentleman; I don't recall his name, but he shouted over to another gentleman and said "he's here for the interview with Givvy." I could hear him say words to the effect of "where the hell is he, did he forget or is he stuck over at the airport. "10 minutes or so passed and the gentlemen in the office came out. He was dressed in a dark grey or blue 2-piece suit with a light blue or white shirt with a dark grey or blue tie. A white man with a slight cockney accent, probably my height of 5"9" or slightly taller and said "Givvy's stuck over at the airport, looks like I'm going to have to interview you" reluctantly, he said to follow him into his office where he started to proceed to interview me.

He asked "so what's your name then" I replied "Rudolph"
He said" Randolph"
I said "Rudolph"
He said "Adolph"
I said "Rudolph / like the reindeer"
He said "Rudolph/ Randolph/ Adolph – we can't have people messing up your name, I'll call you "Rudy", hope you don't mind?" So from that day on, especially in work, people started to call me Rudy, I was known as Rudy from that day and it was that gentleman by the name of Andy Smith, the CEO and founder of priority airfreight that called me they from day one and since then it has stuck.

Within a week, I was at my new job and learning how to do customs entry declarations. If only Meadows had offered the same opportunity, I would probably still be there now. Ha ha! (That was a joke!)

By this time, I had already passed my driving test and had bought my first car. I invested in a ford escort mark 2 that cost me £100.00 – the car was so cheap even for those times that the insurance, 3rd part fire and theft cost me £105.00

The way a looked at it was that it must be a bargain because if my car got burnt out or was stolen for some reason, I would have made a profit of £5.00 – quick math … lol.

The day I bought the car and was driving it home, being a learner driver, obviously, I didn't have much experience on the road. I remember, cautiously, nervously pulling up to the traffic lights, probably looking all suspicious as the police were sitting in the car right next to me. As I pulled off, I stalled the engine so obviously now I was drawing attention to myself.

I started the engine, shifted into 1st gear and nervously started to drive off until the police pulled me over less than 20 meters away.

Nervously cool as I sat there, they both approached my car. One officer stayed on the pavement/kerb side while the other came to my side and tapped on the window for me to roll it down. I rolled down the window, and immediately he asked, "Is this your car?" I said, "Yes." Then he went on to ask a load of other questions like: "How long have you had it?" "Do you have insurance?" "Where did you buy it from?" "How old are you, where do you live?" "Do you have a full driving license? Let me see your license."

I showed him my license and thought everything was in order. Then suddenly, the other officer appeared with a smile on his face and said, with a smirk, "You have four bald tires—four illegal tires that will get you 3 points each. 12 points would mean a year-long ban."

They spoke between themselves and decided that, because I was a new driver, they would cut me some slack. The first officer said, "It's your lucky day." Now there's me thinking they're going to turn a blind eye, give me a caution, and tell me to get new tires. But they didn't. He said, "Son, it's your lucky day. If you get 12 points now, it's an automatic disqualification for 1 year. I'm going to write you up for 11 points so that you don't get the ban."

He then wrote out the producer (the ticket they issue to produce documents) and told me that I had 7 days to produce my driver's license and insurance documents at my local police station. With that, they cheerfully told me to drive safely, jumped into their vehicle, and went about their business.

What a relief I thought, still a little shocked, still a little shaken because I had managed to get away without a ban or a fine but more importantly, I was shocked to even to be told that I was driving a car that had 4 balled tyres, not one or two but 4, why, because I had just purchased the car from my uncle and was literally just driving it home. I've been in that car hundreds of times throughout the years and everything always seemed in order, my uncle always had the car serviced and M.o.t'd (ministry of transport) so you would think nothing wrong with driving the vehicle home that day without issue. However, once I got home, called my uncle and explained to him what happened, he suddenly said, "oh yeah, I was supposed to mention that you had to get the tyres checked out before you go on a long drive"

My first day at Priority. I was given instructions of what time to be in the office and where to park, 2 easy instructions right? Givvy my manager and also the import manager, a small slightly chubby guy with Asian Indian origins, always dressed smart usually smart trousers shirt open collar, no tie, he loved his jewelry, always wore Indian gold that he said either came from India or Dubai. He had a big heart, a big mind, was way sharper and smarter than the average person I'd known, he was way cleverer than given credit for and if somebody didn't know something they should, he would consider them to be an idiot. Givvy told me to be in the office at 04:30 hours which I found strange but wasn't an issue for me because I was such an early bird, I thought it was some kind of test or initiation to see how serious I was about the job but there was real reasoning behind this start time.

So that first day starting at priority air freight it was probably maybe it was around October November time I was given two very clear instructions where to park, Givvy said to park at the far side of the building, the end of building 521, I didn't think he actually meant at the end of the building end where there were about 6 parking spaces, I thought those would be special parking bays for management or something but apparently that's where I was supposed to park. He should have just said that, but he said in the car park so obviously I went looking for the nearest car park at the end of the building which was about a 20 minute walk back to the building.

When I eventually got to the office he said, "why have you taken so long ?" and I told him where I parked, he laughed and said that I went to the wrong place and that I should have parked in the bays literally outside the office block. I would never make that same mistake again; it made me late for the first day. Not a good start I thought.

The days at Priority started early because flights were coming in early and had to be met. What I mean by that is that flights from the far east, mainly Hong Kong, coming in on either the Cathay Pacific CX251 or British Airways BA026 or 028 arrival time anywhere from 04:30 hrs to 07:30 hours meant that goods had to be processed and cleared customs and out to deliver before 09:00 hrs. Priority airfreight weren't just your generic freight forwarder, they specialized in what's known as the courier industry where the courier express services would be prioritized over any general cargo on the same flights. A true definition of known businesses that specialize courier express today would be the likes of DHL, FedEx and UPS, the industry heavyweights but there are many many more even more specialist smaller creative independent organizations also.

The rule was, from wheels down goods had to be handled and turned around from aircraft into the courier facility building (CFL) within 40 minutes. The clearing agents/ us, would all be waiting for the arrival of the goods into the arrival hall of building 139, where we would have access to goods that needed to be examined by a customs officer and/ or if we failed to receive a pre alert by fax overnight, we would have to take the copies that accompanied the goods, complete a customs entry declaration form there and then and present to the authorities there and then.

It was a manual process, so you had to know your stuff. Building 139 was always a part of my history but it wasn't always there known as the courier building. Not sure what the building was used for before CFL but if you worked in a time of building 139, it's something that you'll always be associated with, something that is the cornerstone of most highly respected, successful businesses today, businesses that are market leading giants today that have global acclaim way beyond Heathrow airport Hounslow Middlesex.

Not too far before my time, courier goods would arrive on passenger luggage carousels in the passenger terminals, accompanied by a courier, a person/ individual travelling on a flight with baggage luggage tags assigned to the commercial bags they were accompanying. The goods would normally be packed in courier sacks attached with manifests outlining the content and description of the goods the courier was carrying/ accounting for. For example, the courier would be accompanying 12 courier bags from New York and within those 12 bags/sacks there would be documentation to clear customs and other instructions pertaining to handling of the goods. The courier company would hire an airport porter to retrieve the bags/sacks from the carousels and proceed to goods to declare where met by HM customs and the customs brokers right there and then in the passenger terminal. This process soon outgrows the method, hence the birth of building 139 and the legacy it leaves today.

Everything was done manually as a manual declaration we had no access to computers; it didn't exist, everything was handwritten with duplicate documents between carbon paper for extra copies, formulas calculated by the use of a calculator was the only type of accessory we had to assist us. If you made a mistake, you would have to correct it with type or erase it and start again. We worked fast and accurate, express is the name of the game and being accurate was part and parcel of the service.

Remember I told you I wanted to learn customs and how I wanted to learn how to do customs entry declarations? I thought the entry side of the business was the side of the business that had the longevity, sustainability, especially on the import side of things, I thought then and still do now that the customs entry declaration is the most important and crucial part of the business regardless of everything else going on. Working at Priority I was fast tracked and educated within months of joining the business, I was taught absolutely everything there needed to know about importing goods into the country, specifically for priority airfreight and their clients but I learnt a lot in such a short space of time, the foundation enabled me to enhance my career and remain viable and sustainable within the business for many years.

All good things must come to an end, although I enjoyed my time at priority and most of the people that I worked with were good honest people, although they tried to convince me to stay, my mind was already made up, had it not been for 1 individual, I'd probably stayed a lot longer, but the time was now, I could see a brighter future armed with a wealth of knowledge and a holistic understanding of the industry, although Givvy was happy for me to move on, we'd become close friends during my time there, I was the apprentice and him the mentor, it was a little sad to say my good byes and leave.

F.O.B International... (stepping up and taking responsibility)

At this point I was now familiar with both general air cargo customs declaration and now air courier customs declarations as that was the main process type at Priority Airfreight. I suppose courier clearance was specialist because the process was different to general cargo and only a handful of agents had the ability to clear couriers over hundreds of agents that could clear general cargo only.

I saw the job advertisement for an import courier supervisor so of course I jumped at the opportunity to take the interview, so I went out one lunch time, took the interview and was offered the job there and then, more or less immediately.

F.O.B international was a newer company that Priority where the owners were smart and ambitious, and you could see that they were going places fast. Everything at FOB was quality control first, quick accurate service where the customer was always right. I came into the import department and although I had an import manager, Mark Schmitz, he was very familiar and proficient with general cargo but didn't have a clue about the courier side of the building. I had an understanding of both so that put me in a strong position and gave me the belief that I could do better being here at FOB.

Remember before when I told my boss at Meadows airfreight that one day I'd be driving a company car, well quickly soon after joining FOB, they allowed me to take the escort van home and said that it was my vehicle and would be more convenient and reliable than my own car, which they were right, I was happy to have a new white escort van, to me it was a company car, I was over the moon and felt valued and an early achievement of mine that was proud moment for me.

It was great working there, lots of young people being able to express themselves and being creative and learning at the same time. One guy in particular encouraged me the most, he wasn't that much older than me but always encouraged me to do better and the rewards would come, he said "I'm telling you from experience, they look after you if you work hard and show loyalty" his name, Gary Waters and he was right.

I had the task and responsibility of setting up the import courier department of the business, under the watchful eye of Mark Schmitz but he allowed me to do my own thing as he simply wasn't interested in the courier business. This allowed me to grow more or less as an independent worker and in some aspects, courier was always seen as the short cut unethical way of customs declaration, deemed as second rate clearance compared to the traditional general cargo that had been around for years. Courier clearance in comparison was fairly new, hence not many people knew how to do it let alone understand it. Courier clearance was always my advantage over everyone else and always kept it interesting for me.

For example, knowing how to clear goods through the courier terminals, meant that I had another unique quality that not many others had. Clearing passengers in the arrivals hall was another unique element and another string to my bow that kept things interesting for. This was called M.I.B. Clearance. Not Men In Black, M.I.B stands for "Merchandise in baggage". This is where the customer would arrive in the arrival hall carrying goods/ merchandise in their luggage and would enter the red channel of goods to declare. As a MIB agent, we worked closely with HM Customs, it was like a partnership. Sometimes we would have regular clients that we would know about the arrival times and goods they would be declaring, other times you would go blind not knowing the client or what they were carrying until the last minute. How that worked was because HM Customs had a list of preferred agents/brokers and if you got the phone call from them, would mean they valued and endorsed your services as authentic agents. MTT was the number one MIB agent at the time followed by Greyound, JAG Freight then us FOB. The MIB always seemed like an official job, expertly important because it allowed us to get airside into the customs hall on official business.

I remember I would be walking into the customs hall when passengers were coming through, pass security check feeling like James

Bond secret government agent with my photo ID and briefcase, dressed very casually listening to the whispers of passengers or people in the arrivals hall muttering and uttering amongst themselves, who is that guy, he must be well important. It used to bring a smile to my face. Like I said, we had regular clients and on the off chance there would be some random clients eagerly waiting for me to turn up in the terminal to clear their goods.

Often, they wouldn't know the drill, or they would try their luck and try to sneak through customs without declaring the goods. I used to ask passengers why they would try to sneak through after they've been caught by the customs officers and now being scrutinized with a full baggage check examination, usually it would be "I thought I was within my limits, or I've been on a long flight from New York and I just want to get home."

One particular day, I took a call for a customs officer in terminal 3 saying that he had a Mr. Michael Jackson in the hall that needed assistance from a clearing agent. Obviously that got my attention and I said "are you taking the piss – you have Michael Jackson in the red channel needing clearance" he said "yes, he claims his name is Michael Jackson, not the one that you and I know and he has a scouse accent (Liverpudlian) but he's black" Anyway, this was too good not to drop everything and head over to the terminal. On arrival, there was this tall, heavy-set gentlemen, light skin black complexion similar to mine, looking all nervous and disheveled like he had the world on his shoulders and very much under pressure.

The officer introduced me to Mr. Jackson, I introduced myself and asked what goods he was carrying and that I was here to help. He looked at me and asked how I was going to help him and when I explained the process he seemed a little relieved and more at ease then he said "this customs officer guy threw the book at me and told me that I would be facing fines and even imprisonment for failing to declare goods, he said that it was defrauding the crown, smuggling, tax invasion, he really game he a hard time, that's why I was looking so nervous, he asked if I had a clearing agent, I didn't know what that was so obviously I said no, he said well you need one before you can leave the building or you will be detained along with your goods" he said, as you could imagine, that freaked me out, I was shitting myself – then you walked in, looking casually relaxed, black like me, you're one of us, you instantly made me feel at ease but how you gonna help me again?"

I explained the process again and within the hour, he was processed and cleared and out the building on route to Woodgreen Westbury Avenue north London where his store was located. I believe their store was called the avenue. Over time they would get to use my services regularly, both he and his business partner Robert Henry would use my services over the years and would also refer their friends and business colleagues in their industry to use my services also. The Avenue in Peckham Rye southeast London, Dark N Cold soho London, PHLIP, kings road London, Sunplash Nottingham, Dnzo Streatham south London, Dub Vendor Clapham junction London, Jet star NW London, Cousins Records Tottenham, Rock Fort records, Mitcham, street life north London amongst many many more that came my way due to word of mouth referrals mostly. I got a reputation for being the clearing agent for trendy fashion / street wear was what we use to call it and music, vinyl Records and CDs mainly. Businesses and individuals would just find me, I never advertised and never turned business away, it was an amazing feeling that so many individuals and businesses knew my name personally and would only want to deal with me, it was amazingly awesome, I felt I found my purpose…

Working at FOB felt like excitement every day, there was always a bit of drama on workdays and workdays were 7 days a week. Working everyday was part and parcel of the job. The airport was open every day and flights arrived and departed every day, so nothing stopped. Meeting flights in the morning all day through til the night made it extra specially exciting, you would get to see everything and get to know everybody, your job was your job, and you had the responsibility to carry out your tasks and be held accountable for mistakes. So, you either made few or no mistakes or you knew how to cover the mistake, so nothing ever became an issue.

There was so much to talk about at my time with FOB that it would probably take another book to go through the whole FOB experience but what I will do is cover a few moments/ highlights that stand out in my mind as significant memories at that particular time.

The first and second time I travelled outside of the UK was with my father and the older sister Jacqui when I was 6 years old my father took me and Jacqui back to the island of st kitts in the Caribbean the island of his birth, the first time returning since he left in the 50's and the second time was approx. 6 years later when we visited his sisters auntie Dolly & auntie Joanie and uncle Winston in Canada. We never travelled overseas as a family back then because there were six of us and was way too expensive for all of us to travel at the same time. Thinking about it, we didn't even do staycation family holidays, maybe go to the beach for the say but holiday, nah, in the summer holidays, we usually stayed at home and played locally with other kids in the same situation to our hearts content.

However, because of our international travel to st kitts and Canada, I had a passport, so to my surprise when I walked into the office one morning and the export manager Simon asked if anyone had a passport and was available to travel in 2 hours, I said I have a passport but I have work to do, flights to meet etc; Simon said, don't worry, this is more important, we need you to go to New York and make 3 hand deliveries in manhattan. My ears sprung up and eyes wide open, I replied, New York, New York City, you want me to go to New York?, yes he said, "can you go to the airport now or do you need to get your passport from home?" I literally had to go home immediately and get back to board the flight for a 10:30 hrs departure time which I made in good time, I was now sitting on the airplane 18 years of age, travelling alone to New York representing the company and it felt great, literally as if I was on top of the world.

Sitting on that plane all I could think about was that I was going to New York, the big apple, the home of hip hop and everything else associated with it. Being 18 in the late 80's and hip hop and rap music took your interest, the obvious place to be New York. It's a place I always wanted to visit as a kid because we had so much American tv broadcasting in the UK, influencing styles and trends I couldn't wait to get there, even if it was a quick turnaround, no overnight stay, strictly in and out no messing around.

My instructions were as follows – "you have 3 drops to make in the twin towers. Morgan Stanley, Morgan Grenfell and Salomon Brothers. Make sure you make the flight PA 103 (Panam 103), when you arrive take a yellow cab, an official taxi, go directly to manhattan to the twin towers and get the driver to wait for you while you make your deliveries. After each delivery ask to use the phone and call us here in the office with verbal proof of delivery but make sure you get them to sign the document as actual proof of delivery because that's how we get paid. Make sure you get in the right elevator as the building is huge and each company will probably be on different floors and different floors have different elevators" I was handed a couple hundred pounds £'s and off I went and there I was.

The driver waited for me as I made all three drops. I was to make the drops asap to give enough time to get back to the airport to take the same flight back to London that I arrived on. The same plane but the flight number had changed, the Panam 102 (PA102). I wasn't supposed to pay the driver until he dropped me back to the airport but then suddenly, the driver turned off the road and into the petrol station (they call it the gas station) and asked if I could pay him some of the fare money early because he needed fuel to get me back to the airport. At this point I got a little anxious for the first time being in New York as right now I didn't really know what to think. Watching all that American TV, was I about to be robbed, kidnapped or worse? Anyway, I handed over twenty dollars to the driver filled up the tank and we were back on track and in route to JFK.

So, I'm now back at the airport waiting in the departure lounge thinking I wish I had the time to spend in New York for at least one night. Put it this way, I wouldn't be disappointed if the flight was cancelled and had to be put up in a hotel for the night.

While I was waiting, I decided to take a look around the airport shops and remembered that Ellen, a lady that worked as the receptionist and secretary to the directors of FOB asked me if I could pick up a copy of the book "Spy Catcher" because she couldn't buy it in the UK. Apparently, it was banned in the UK because the book was an autobiography and told a few secrets about the British government https://en.wikipedia.org/wiki/Spycatcher.

I bought 2 or 3 copies with some of the money that I had left then took a wonder over to Macdonald's for a burger, fries and root beer, watch a bit of TV then decided to treat myself to a Budweiser. At that time, Budweiser beer wasn't available in the UK so I decided I would be the first one out of my friends to try one.

"Can I have a Budweiser please" I asked.

"You have ID buddy" the bartender asked.

"Yes" as I handed over my passport and grinned showing all my teeth looking forward to the first sip.

He said "how old are you"

Confidently proud I responded "18"

He continued to say, "you got to be 21 to drink in here son – the kiddies' sodas are over on that counter"

I said: "you can drink alcohol when you're 18 in the UK,"

He said "Well you're not in the UK now and I'm not prepared to lose my license over some kids that want to drink a man's beer."

He laughed as I turned away in disappointment and settled for a sprite instead. (To think I've been drinking since I was 14 in the UK, it was normal, plus, Budweiser weren't as strong as some of our UK beers)

Lockerbie – devastated –

https://en.wikipedia.org/wiki/Pan_Am_Flight_103

This is crazy, it's absolutely incredible to think about it but literally 3 weeks before this disaster, I was actually on the same plane that was blown up over Lockerbie. To make it worse, just like how I was asked if I had a passport and was willing to fly to New York randomly as a courier, this was a regular occurrence in the industry and the industry were in the business to offer cheap flight across the Atlantic to general members of the public. For example, if you wanted to go on holiday at cost-effective price, you would sign up as a courier and travel with the manifest of the courier bags/ goods you were representing. So, as business we/ F.O.B. shared our USA traffic. Inbound /outbound with another courier company called Abacus. The story goes, students, boyfriend and girlfriend were looking to get away to the USA and the cheaper way to travel would be to fly by courier.

As we only needed a courier per flight, the plan was for the guy to go first and that his girlfriend would follow on the next flight the next day. On this particular day, it was the Abacus staff that would give the couriers their instructions and dispatch them to the airport. One of the drivers explained to me at a later date that he watched the couple hug and kiss and overheard parts of their conversation and how they couldn't wait to see each other again tomorrow to start their holiday together. I think they were taking a gap year out of university or something like that. They said their goodbyes and were never reunited in New York because a short while after takeoff, the airplane exploded and crashed over land and destroying everything in it and beneath it, what a tragedy. Immediately this was all over the news, the airspace came to a halt, we were all obviously stunned into silence, and I could stop but think about it could have been me on that flight or one of my colleagues.

A sad sad time. Over the following days and weeks, the directors of the company and many other courier companies that had freight on that aircraft had to visit the site in Lockerbie to identify goods and articles that belonged to the company. This is now a criminal investigation on the scale of a terrorist attack and one that changed lives forever, airport transport security would never be the same ever again, the world changed that day when Panam 103 blow up and Panama never required from that devastation and was eventually bankrupt as an airline.

The big Red Dove. (it was massive!)

When I started at FOB and after a short while they handed me the keys to the ford escort van, one of the reasons I was happy to drive it and take it home overnight was because unlike the other company vehicles, this one had no logo on the side, no company name, no advertising and it suited me fine because I just wanted to blend in away from the office, especially if I was parking at home where the vehicle would be parked on the road and I didn't want to bring any attention to myself of what I did for a living and attract some unwanted unsavoury incidents. I liked the fact that the vehicle was simply all white where I could just blend in and stay under the radar. My boss had other ideas, I get it now but I didn't get it then, in my eyes I was trying to protect the business rather than expose it to the world in which I lived and highlight the fact that we were actually a premium courier company that operated 24/7 and the likelihood of carrying goods in the vehicle overnight was quite possible.

The boss was more interested in advertising and because the van was always mobile, what better way to advertise the business than on your own vehicles. Pretty standard stuff, right? The problem is, F.O.B's logo was this big, massive red dove, it was gigantic, so now there was no way that this vehicle would blend in anywhere.

I argued the point with my both then John Clarke, he was having none of it, he said "when it's your business and your own the van, you decide what you do with it, until then, you do as I say or you can find yourself another job, he went onto to say I'm not having you dictate to me what I can and can't do" From that day, my cards were marked, this was one of many petty incidents where in hindsight even though I thought I was right, I was probably in the wrong, I wasn't experienced enough to put up an argument that

I couldn't win, I just thought they had it in for me whenever I made a good suggestion and looking back now, it was the immature me that didn't really have a clue about business, I thought I knew everything, I know I was a good operator and could get the job done, I supposed looking back now, because I was such a good working and I used to get a lot of praise for my work, I suppose in a way it all went to my head and I took it for granted that I wouldn't be questioned and get away with most things, sometimes I knew I was taking the piss but if it wasn't challenged, well good for me and if it was challenged, the problem was them, not me. I literally stood my ground at the best of times, some would call it arrogance, but I like to refer to it as confidence.

Many years later when I started CCL, John Clarke started another business called Paramount where he hired my services so this time he became the customer, we had a great working relationship, I suppose he felt comfortable dealing with me knowing that I would give me all and even though a little confrontational, I was honest with it, integral and confident with it, I guess he either liked me as a person or respected the way that I work or both.

Nigel Fox (Foxy to his mates)

I had a situation with a member of staff from Abacus couriers, a client partner to F.O.B, we collaborated with them on many projects.

For example, we would do all their imports and because most of their imports were based around courier operations, 9 times out of 10, they had to deal with me. One particular day, it was a midweek day, not sure which, can't remember, but I remember everything being delayed from the start of the day all the way through to the night.

There are a number of reasons why airports get congested, flights can't land or take off, a number of reasons that could do with the weather or even worse, the flights going technical is a term used then there is a problem with an aircraft, and it cannot take off for some reason. I worked from very early in the morning to the evening, covering both shifts as there were people off in the office and it was common to do double shifts, it wasn't really a problem, that's the way we worked. Anyway, on this particular day, all inbound flights were being delayed and this guy from Abacus was constantly on my case basically telling me that I didn't know what I was doing and that I was making life difficult for him. He didn't believe me when I told him on one particular occasion that the flight from New York was delayed due to bad weather conditions, another time I told him that some freight from Dublin had gone missing and the airlines would contact me when found, he thought I was lying about everything then he called me lazy and unprofessional and that he would have a word with my boss and id be sacked in the morning.

Ah man, this dude was pushing all my buttons, but I wasn't budging, I didn't bite back, I simply kept me professional conduct and explained and advised what I knew but he wasn't listening to me, wasn't listening to a word I had to say and as far as he was concern, I was an idiot. Anyway, that was that this all happened earlier in the day, and I knew that he would be off shift soon so I wouldn't have to deal with him again that day. Low and behold, like me, he was covering both shifts so to my surprise when we were both still working at 8pm in the evening and I called their office to tell them that the flight from Amsterdam had been delayed due to a problem with air traffic control or something, he blew his top, shouting and screaming, swearing and calling me all the names under the sun saying things like you're definitely getting fired in the morning and it would be his pleasure. With that, he slammed the phone down and cut me off in mid-sentence.

OK, I've just given you the back story, painted a picture and created the scene. I was like, "nah man, he didn't – he didn't just hang up on me – he didn't just slam the phone down on me while I was trying to explain" he did, and I was livid. I remember pacing up and down my office, punching my clenched fist into the open one, talking to myself in disbelief contemplating what to do and this guy had really got under my skin, and I wasn't about to let it slide. In my mind, he needed to understand that somethings are out of my control and I'm trying my best here. I thought, okay, let me call him back because he probably didn't even know that I was talking when I was cut off in mid-sentence, so I'd give him the benefit of the doubt. I called their office and asked to speak to Nigel Fox. I think I've spoken to him briefly one time before, he hadn't worked there for that long, so I wasn't really familiar with him, had no relationship with him but wanted to make things right. Someone else answered the phone and I could hear them say "Foxy, F.O.B is on the phone" he came to the phone and said something like "What the fxxx do you want?" And hung up again.

I immediately called back, got him on the phone again and immediately said "don't hang up on me when I'm trying to explain something to you "and guess what, he did it again, he put the phone down at his end with me and at this point I was more than livid.

I was raging literally at boiling point. Without hesitation, I grabbed the van keys now on route to the abacus office which was about 2 miles down the road, I'm now at the warehouse door and being greeted by other staff members that I know and they're asking me what's wrong which I reply "where's Foxy" to which he's pointed out to me so I proceed to where he was sitting at a desk at the back of the warehouse and shouted "are you Foxy" he replied "Yes, who's asking?" I said "that fxxxxxx idiot you keep putting the phone down to from F. OB" to which, I grabbed him around the neck and continued to lift him from his chair from behind his desk until I had to be dragged off by 2 members of staff because apparently, I was choking him to death. Not my greatest moment but a memorable one. As I let go and he fell to the floor in a slump, I said "don't ever put the phone down on me again ", called him a few names under the sun then promptly left the building.

As I calmed down, I thought well, definitely getting fired now. That night, because of all the delays, I finished up work way after midnight into the early hours. When I got back into the office the following morning, John Clarke the CEO/managing Director, Paul McCarthy a founder partner and Director and Roger Painter the other director were all waiting for me in the office obviously not very happy drinking tea.

John said, before I sack you, I need you to tell me what happened, he went onto say that their CEO wasn't very happy about the situation and that we were lucky that they didn't call the police and press charges because apparently, I was out of control. "So, what happened Rudee?" John asked; "well Mr. Clarke" I said, first I apologize for my conduct, it was very unprofessional of me, and it won't happen again, then I continued to reenact the turn of events in detail leaving nothing out, the whole build up during the day and keeping calm then I flipped. John said "who do you think you are? This is a place of business, this isn't the streets you know, you can't just go around strangling people without consequences"

I apologies again. There was a long silence in the room until Roger Painter said, "what you did was wrong, but I could understand why you did what you did" then he looked at Paul and said "what do you think Paul" he sighed for a second, paused the said "I would hit him again" and laughed. John said "this ain't no laughing matter" at which Paul responded, yes, you're right but you can't sack the kid over it, he made a mistake and he's apologized so let's consider this a warning and if anything like this happens again then we'll terminate his employment then" You could see that John especially wasn't happy about it but more importantly I wasn't sacked yet, Paul and Roger voted against it but deep down I don't think John wanted to fire me anyway otherwise it would have been done already. I was dismissed, returned to my duties relived on my reflection, grateful to the board for not firing me but also appreciating the decision could have gone the other way, then what? I loved this job; I liked the people and loved the atmosphere. It was a job that was made for me like no other and I could have screwed it up over some ego nonsense.

Lessons learnt, onwards and upwards. – Never sacrifice your integrity over ego -

Arsenal 89, Liverpool.-

https://en.wikipedia.org/wiki/1988%E2%80%9389_Arsenal_F.C._season

I've always been an avid fan of Arsenal football club, but I think this year, was the year, the turning point that injected the love for the club into me more than ever. Let me set the scene, although I supported the club from a young age, I never saw the team play live, always on TV or highlights on match of the day but never live. Not because I didn't want to but more due to the fact that I played a lot of sports that always coincided with match day, usually on a Saturday or a midweek evening. When I got older and started working, my working life was hectic. Now working around the clock, 7 days a week, where was the time to go to a football match let alone listen to a game on the radio. Besides, when I was younger there is no way on earth that I would be able to afford a match ticket, let alone season ticket then as I got older, although I was able to buy a match day or season ticket, I couldn't get to the games anyway as I previously explained.

It was the last game of the season and Arsenal, and Liverpool were joint leaders on the same points or something like that but what I did know is that Arsenal had to beat Liverpool by 2 clear goals to become champions.

The game was midweek probably on a Wednesday and an evening kickoff. Everybody wanted to watch this game. The smallest room with the smallest tv became the venue. The room was the security guards' box in building 139 and the screen was his miniature black and white tv with a dodgy pull up Ariel.

It felt like the whole airport stopped working for 90 minutes while that game was being played, freight wasn't being offloaded or loaded onto aircrafts, goods were not being cleared through customs, trucks, vans, cars and bikes were parked up, we were all caught up fun the tension as the first ball was kicked.

I don't want to go through the commentary of the whole game from start to Finnish, I will spare you the details but the magnitude and significant of this game was bigger than football. It appeared as if the whole world had stopped watching this game, nothing else mattered as we crammed around that security hut, nervous as hell, excitement filled with adrenaline and praying for a miracle to happen. It happened, our prayers were answered, as if it was the last kick of the game, Arsenal already one nil up went along to score the second goal, Michael Thomas was the hero, and Arsenal went onto win the title. For all Arsenal fans, the place erupted and the celebrations went into the night as normal business started to resume. Most Liverpool fans were gracious in defeat and for the neutrals, what a game, for arsenal fans, incredible, I still remember it like yesterday.

I had a lot of stuff going on in my life. I was very active, always doing something, involved in something creative or more entrepreneurial. I was still involved with Karate, football, of course I had all my social activities to keep up with and I also had a good few years of being a recording artist and a performing entertainer. At this point of my day job working career, I decided that I needed a change from F.O.B international and because of my connections in the industry, friends of mine at Marken international encouraged me to take a job there which I eventually did but it didn't last long.

Marken International… (quick visit) (Mark & Ken)

My time at Marken was a good one but also a valuable one. You see, when I worked for F.O.B I was more or less running the show, I was more or less in charge of me and worked my schedule around the flight arrival times and that worked well, they just let me get in with it. FOB had more flight activity during the day from the early hours of the morning to very late at night, that was me, keeping busy, now at Marken, they had sporadic flight, the first flight being ex JFK approx. around 7 or 8 am in the morning with a few European flights in between, Amsterdam, Brussels, Paris then at midday they would have the big one coming in from Los Angeles where most of the activity would be done. I found the work relatively easy at Marken and thought the only way to progress there would be if I got a promotion. Although I liked the people, the organization and everything, it just wasn't enough for me, so I decided to leave.

My good mate who sadly passed away a few years ago, Jon Stevens tried to encourage me to stay. I told him I appreciated him putting in a good word to get me the job in the first place but unfortunately, I needed more. He said words to me like I think you're making a mistake, and you should hang on for a while as things change here quickly as Marken was a trendy operation and growing at a rapid pace with lots of young people like me learning the trade.

So, I left Marken with regret, but I had to move on and do me. A few weeks later, Jon approached me one day and said with a smile, the senior management of Marken and the 2 directors were asking questions about why you left because they had you nominated and up for promotion, to take over and run the import department because Dave Maryon was promoted elsewhere and that's the main reason you were hired in the first place. "Well, nobody told me I said, even when I made my feelings clear at the time nobody said anything" had I known at the time of course I would have stayed, it was a great place to work but like I said, I felt the career path was blocked. Mark Adams, one of the directors, then called me and tried to convince me to come back. I thought about it, but it was too late. I made my decision to leave so I was sticking to it. In my mind, they should have tried harder than when I was still employed with them, not wait for me to leave before making the offer. I appreciated the call but at the same time felt undervalued and disrespected, so I politely declined.

Mark remains one of my mentors today. Over the years since leaving Marken and developing my career path Mark has become a good friend of mine, both him and Ken Powell the other director have helped me throughout the years, but it's Mark that me and my family are closest to, and he remains a friend, mentor and confidant to this day.

I thought long and hard about the next move, I did the big company, I did the smaller companies learning lessons from both. Still in contact with my first supervisor Della from Meadows Airfreight, I knew that meadows had been sold/taken over, there was a merger/acquisition or something and even though I don't remember how it exactly went, eventually meadows was to become part of Burlington Air express who eventually changed names to Bax Global or Baxi. There was an opening in the import department, and I decided to go for the job.

HICS – That pay rise conversation –

So, I now find myself in the bosses' office at HICS negotiating a deal onto of the deal that I just negotiated for myself. HICS was set up predominately for inbound customs brokerage surrounding airfreight. The owner/boss Paul Burness was previously the import manager at Skynet UK (Sky Courier) I'm not quite sure how it happened, but Sky supported Paul to establish the business HICS. I'm not sure if they were shareholders in HICS but what I did know was that HICS handled all of Sky's clearance which was very apparent and made a lot of sense. This was the foundation for HICS to grow and develop into the success that it became. I like to think that I was a part of that success. I was only there for a short while compared to some that have been employed there for decades, I'll get back to that later.

The good thing about Paul was that he was a decent man, a fair man most of the time, a friendly all round good guy, I never had any problems with him apart from 3 times, possibly more but these are the encounters that I remember because they left a mark on me for obvious reasons that I'm going to go into. Apart from these 3 incidents, he was always good to me and supported me when and where he could. So, I find myself in Paul's office discussing the company car situation. He supplied all his employees with a company vehicle and all of them were red Citroen box cars/ a car that looked like a miniature van that was really ugly looking and I didn't like it. I made up my mind there and then that I'd rather buy my own car and drive it rather than drive that vehicle.

I don't remember the exact year but these were the times when the UK government were encouraging businesses and individuals to buy diesel vehicles with an incentive of cheaper fuel to petrol and minimum or no road tax and the a company could award an employee a van and that employees wouldn't have to pay any personal tax on the vehicle because it was classified as a fleet van and not a company car. Also, the type of work that was involved, occasionally we would be expected to collect goods/ freight from the airport and deliver to the customer, so again it made sense. I understood all that, but I wasn't feeling any of it, I simply didn't want to be driving that vehicle, it looked ugly and sounded like a tractor, wasn't for me.

I argued my case that I didn't want to drive that vehicle, and he asked me why and I was honest and explained my rationale. He wasn't about to accept my argument, so I approached it a different way. I said ok, what about if you give me the money equivalent to what you were going to give me as a perk (the amount of the car) and I go out and find my own vehicle, he asked what type of vehicle I had in mind and I explained that I wouldn't mind a Vauxhall Astra hatch back where if necessary, the back seats would drop down if I had to carry any goods for delivery. He sighed, hummed and arrhhed for a while then eventually he said, sounds reasonable – okay, sounds like a plan, sounds like a good idea and he agreed for me to purchase the Astra instead.

The whole discussion into negotiation took about half an hour but it felt a lot longer at the time. At first I didn't know if I should ask, I thought, well nobody else has another vehicle so what makes me think he'll agree to my conditions. All said and done, at the end of the day, if you don't ask, you don't get, so I asked the question and got want I wanted. That was the first and hardest time I had discussions with Paul, after all he was the founder and managing director, I was only an import customs broker clerk, only been employed that week and yet I was making demands. I remember a day or two before telling one of my coworkers Charlie what I was planning to do. He said that Paul would never agree with it because he was too tight but then I came back and told him that he agreed to purchase an Astra, Charlie couldn't believe it and asked if I'd threatened Paul jokingly because that's something that he would put money on Paul would never do. I think Charlie was impressed with my negation skills and said: "Fair play, Rude boy!"

It felt good to me, that I had put my foot down and stuck to my guns, although trivial, it felt like a victory, I wasn't going along with being dictated to and settle for the status quo like everyone, I respected Paul for that I know he admired my approach and the respect I thought was mutual.

As soon as I knew that I was joining HICS, I was in contact with a few of my old customers from my time at FOB. I continued to grow my own client base and enhance the reputation I had established previously and now business was really picking up on my own portfolio through word-of-mouth referrals alone. My portfolio of clients would become in-house customers to HICS, so it was evidently obvious how much money I was bringing into the business all regular and all settled by cash. Paul took umbrage to this, not sure why but he did, then one day it slipped.

He approached me as I was dropping off some paperwork in the office and more or less said to me that he didn't like the clients that I kept because they always pay cash and that he wasn't sure if the businesses were legit or not. Most of my clients were black business owners, the majority of my clients base was black, I think he had an issue with how it would look from the outside, it unsettled him for some reason. Back then, more people were becoming entrepreneurs setting up businesses mainly in retail fashion and anything trendy. Small to medium size enterprises was my main focus, I would give them a bespoke service so that they compete with the big boys, and they seemed to like it. Paul thought the profile of that business was to flash and "URBAN" and wasn't sure if it was the right image for HICS. I thought, they pay their bills, what's the problem. right? We never spoke about it again, but a line had been crushed and it didn't sit well with me.

The contradiction still makes me cringe to this day as I tell the story. I approached the boss for a pay rise. It's very obvious why I felt entitled to the pay increase because I was bringing in a lot of business for the company. Not only was I covering my own salary and the car allowance, but also the business that I was bringing in was contributing to a healthy financial situation for the company and improving the bottom line.

Paul had a bit of a stutter, so bear with me, the conversation took longer than necessary so it gave me time to think about my answers before actually saying what I was thinking.

Me:	"Boss – I think you need to give me a pay rise"
Boss:	"Why do you think I need to give you a pay rise, let me think about it"
Me:	"If you need to think about giving me a pay rise, I need to think about leaving"
Boss:	"why would you want to leave?"
Me:	"because"

I didn't even think it was even necessary to explain myself, I thought he was taking liberties, taking the piss to be precise. With that I walked out of the office feeling disrespected and never to return. I left the business the next day. You may ask, why didn't you hang around and wait for him to say yes or no, good point. At the time, what was running through my head was you obviously know that I bring in a lot of business, you obviously know why I'm asking for a pay rise and yet you choose to toy with me. I wasn't accepting that, I was already slightly wounded from the comments he had made previously about the profile of my client portfolio, when it comes to departing with the money that they paid you in cash, all of a sudden, it's worth something.

It wasn't exactly a rash decision taken in hast, A couple months before I'd be talking to several clients and in a hypothetical situation, if I was to leave HICS, would they follow me, to the ones that I spoke to the resounding and unanimous reply was YES, so it was already embedded in my thinking when I had that last discussion with Paul.

I remember packing my things up into a plastic carrier bag, didn't keep many things at work, and saying goodbye to my coworkers, they thought I was joking. Charlie asked me if I was serious, I said yes, and he went onto say that I was crazy and that I would have regrets. I told him that I was starting my own business and that he was welcome to join me, Charlie looked at me as if I was a mad man then tried to convince me to stay one last time then resigned to the fact and wished me all the best and said, "see you around Rude boy!" I replied, "you might want to consider joining me", he laughed it off, I laughed it off then a few weeks passed when Charlie called me and asked if the offer was still on the table.

I thought I might have inspired him, whatever the reason, we were now to become business partners, on our way to building our empire and doing things our way. In the last 30 years or so, HICS staff retention has been fairly solid, especially at senior management level. The funny story is about the guy that replaced me at HICS a guy called Mark Manders, he's still there to this day, to this day, I know he took over the Astra, I wonder if he's still driving it, ha-ha! This was probably early 90's a long time ago, it always puts a smile on my face when I tell that story. :)

Life was good at J.A.G freight (until you see the true colours)

I enjoyed my time at J.A.G but all good things come to an end. Within the 7 years or there, a lot can happen in 7 years, lots of toing and froing, people coming and going, building bonds and fall outs but most importantly being true to yourself and making the right decisions for you.

Charlie had left the business and went onto become the founder owner of his own business "CBS" (Customs Brokerage Services)

Charlie's departure was aided by some kind of disagreement between him and J.A.G's owners Pat and Jim Galvin, nothing to do with me what so ever but I was thrown into the middle of it all and asked to make a decision. Because me and Charlie were partners, everyone obviously thought that I would opt to leave with Charlie, I didn't want to leave at that time, I had my own opinions, my own way of dealing with things, I was my own man and decided to stay. CBS went onto be a great success story and Charlie and myself remain friends to this day, no way as close as we were before but there's mutual respect and admiration on both sides.

Getting back to all good things come to an end, it was time to leave JAG.

I was grateful for that opportunity to be able to come together in partnership with another business where they recognized the skill set that I had as an operator with the ability to sell and market myself in a fashion that attracted consistent business. For others to recognize that and want to go into business with you, to me, that's a remarked thing. I learnt never to take myself for granted and never let anyone else take you for granted in and out of business. We attract what we put out and I'm happy to be able to of had that experience and now it was time to move on but not everyone saw it that way...

JAG – treatment –

Summer 1998 still at JAG having lunch with a couple of colleagues. Small talk with Brian Kelly, Bryan Nuttycombe and Sean O'Farrell.

We would talk about life in general, family, work, goals dreams and aspirations then onto more serious topics like how we could help to support the business and make it more attractive to customers. We all felt a part of the business, we felt as if we had a shared valued interest in that business and we all worked well together, we all got on as people, the vibes were always good in the office and the 4 of us just bonded with a common goal to do better. I'm not even sure where the idea came from or even how the conversation started, who mentioned what first, I don't know I have no idea but we were sitting there eating lunch and having a laugh, then I said, that's not a bad idea. Suddenly the discussion went from football on the weekend to fast cars and the cost of living to "we should start our own business, take control of our lives and do better" The conversation stopped in its tracks for a short second, the pause didn't last long, and it was more or less shrugged off and somebody said," lunch is over, let's get back to work"

That thought stuck with me over the following days and weeks ahead until we spoke about it again. This time, it was a more serious conversation taking up most of the lunch break, which was usually around an hour. Everyone had contributed to the conversation and instantly knew that they had all been thinking about what I had been thing about over the last couple of weeks. This was all very much still talk but we did manage to come up with a company name and we certainly established the business profile with each founder members role and responsibility. I was to head the sales drive and business development as a strength and concentrate on operations. Brian was to oversee operations, Sean was to be regulatory, and compliance and Bryan was to be head of financial affairs because apparently, he used to work for Barclays Bank.

The strategy was to be an independent, neutral customs broker, catering for UK businesses that had no budget to house their own customs brokerage department and we also had a very niche name for the services we would offer. Sean came up with the name as he took a swig of his can of coke and said "it's obvious – we should call it Customs Clearance Limited – CCL has a nice ring to it "and there you go, immediately the name was established, everything was made to feel a lot more realistic, this could really happen, we could actually be doing this.

I know I've been a company owner before, but this felt different with more experience under my belt, This time I felt ready to do something special, It wasn't a knee jerk or anything like that, to start this new project with a bunch of people that I've worked with for at least 6 of the last 7 years, felt like the right thing to do as we planned our way ahead and had regular catch ups on the subject, we knew what we had to do if we wanted to make this a reality but nobody, including me was 100% ready to make that leap into the unknown because we were secure in our job roles, the company paid us well, we all had nice company cars, enjoyed the job and the people we worked with so our conversations kind of fizzled out over the coming weeks and wasn't really discussed again but played on my mind even more.

I was ambitious, become even more so over the years and even more determined to want to do better and level up. It was time to move on, but I wanted to plan the right move rather than jump into a move or be pushed into a move, so it was obvious to me that setting up CCL was the answer, the only way to go. Regardless of anyone else joining me, I was determined to make this move but it was all about timing. This is something I had to do, my heart was set on it, I figured I'm not getting any younger and if anything was going to happen, it would have to be soon, I mean as soon as by the end of the year. By now, I was having serious thoughts and thinking again of all the clients that would follow me if I made the move alone then contemplating if all 4 of us made the move, how many customers would we secure. At the end of the day, all said and done, I'm responsible for me so that's how my thought process started to unfold, everything else on top would be a bonus right?!

Anyway, later that year my grandfather, my father's father passed away in St. Kitts and I was back there for the funeral. It was a big funeral with the majority of my family there flying in from all parts of the world to pay respects. Under the circumstances, it was good to be back amongst family and also a reflective time for me personally. I needed to do better, had to do better and level up. I wanted to enjoy whatever time left I had on this earth and wanted to be in a position to do things on my terms. Win, lose or draw had to be on my terms, my decision, my way. It was clear, so it was thought, so it was said, so it was written, so it shall be done. The plan was to hand my notice in on my return from the Caribbean, but you know how it works, nothing quite goes according to plan when you have so many other things going on in your life. The end of '98 came and went in a flash and during this time things were getting serious between me and my girlfriend Lesa.

Things were good, life was good, we were happy and planning to spend the rest of our lives together even if nothing was spoken about or we didn't make any plans to, we just knew it was going to be as we were so comfortable together and shared a lot of things in common. From the first time we met, I knew she was the one. She was so beautifully elegant with a nice smile that caught my immediate attention.

I just knew we'd be together someday, and I was prepared to

pursue it until I got a yes or a No. Luckily for me it was a yes. Ha-ha ! There was no need to upset the apple cart, no need to rock the boat by handing in my notice, not now when things felt so good in life, right, wrong, I still had that niggly feeling chipping away at me so I opened the discussions again with my coworkers to put everything in perspective, to test the mood and see if this was something that we could all do together. Everyone was still all positive about tidbit nobody really wanted to take that leap into the unknown, so the idea was shelved again.

It's funny how fate has a way or shows up when you least expect it.

I was away visiting family in Canada. On my return, the next day I went into the office feeling all positive about life and feeling good about myself. Put it this way, before I went away, I got wind/ I heard through the grape vine that another business was about to make a move on one of our top clients and make them an offer/ a deal that they couldn't refuse. I heard about this and thought of approaching the client as I knew them fairly well and now one of my old friends was also the import manager and I wanted to reassure him that their business was in the best care with us over any other offer put on the table. I tried to set up a meeting with him but I was going away before he could see me, so I asked Brian to go instead and I even told him what to say.

Fate plays a part in our lives; I believed it then and believe it today more than ever. Things happen for a reason, we often question the negative and not the positive, we cherish the good and dismiss the bad. You have the back story; I gave Brian his instructions. I told him to meet the import manager (who's my friend), let him know how important a client they are to us, discuss their account and ask him what it would take to secure the business. Knowing the client and the manager like I do, in my mind it was a done deal, a full gone conclusion. In my head it was more of an appreciation to let the customer know how valuable they are to us and we do not take them for granted but obviously understanding there would be offers from other businesses as they ran an attractive business and would be a nice account for most.

This is what happened. Brian was accused of offering Steve the import manager a bribe. You see, Steve had left the business some years before but then came back to the business with more experience as the import manager and was only a few weeks in. Steve and Brian had never done business before, even though they had spoken on the phone, they didn't know each other like that. Whereas I knew Steve personally as a friend and had done business with him before over the years, we grew up in the industry together. Unfortunately, Steve is no longer with us. May God rest his soul in eternal peace. The instruction was clear, but God knows what happened there. They met, Steve thought he was being set up and feeling uneasy about the situation reported the incident to his boss who in turn called a meeting with our boss that led to Brian being sacked on the spot.

I could see Brians charcoal grey Volkswagen Golf in the car park and was anxious to ask him how the meeting went with Steve. I was especially looking forward to hearing how he'd secured the business. I parked my car and went upstairs into the office. As I approached my desk and greeted everyone good morning, I knew something was wrong but couldn't work out what exactly. I sat down in a tense atmosphere thinking to myself about what happened, what I had done. The office was unusually quiet, so silent you could hear a pin drop and as a looked around and couldn't see Brian anywhere, I asked "Where's Brian?" Tim the office manager said, "oh, don't you know? you better go and speak to Pat and Jim!"

At that point I expected the worst, what the hell had happened, what's happened to Brian.

I sat down in Pat and Jims office as Jim started to explain what happened. It wasn't actually an explanation; it was more like a statement. He proceeded to say that he fired Brian because he offered the client a bribe to take the business. My head sunk into my hands then I immediately lifted my head and explained to Jim that I heard rumour that another company was going after the business and because I was going on holiday, I asked Brian to take the meeting instead and that he wasn't here to bribe the business away but more to secure the business. Jim said that he didn't dent anteing, so he had no choice but to sack him on the spot. Brian left the business the day before I got back.

I called him at home and explained that I had a discussion with Jim, and he told me what happened. I asked him why he didn't explain himself properly, he went onto say I tried to talk but he wouldn't let me have my say and I felt there was no trust, his mind was already made up and he wanted me gone so I went. I asked what happened to Steve, how was the meeting. Brian thought it was a good meeting and felt that it went well and wasn't sure why they thought a bribe was in question. That's still the mystery to this day but also the catalyst and spear head to ignite project CCL as I thought JAGs handling of the whole situation was very unprofessionally one sided, with some prejudice and way out of order that confirmed to me that I could no longer work for these people when they had just terminated a good guy's contract and feeling smug about it, that didn't sit well with me. I was fuming and made my feelings very clear, all Jim kept on saying was he didn't deny it so he must be guilty.

I called an emergency meeting with Brian and invited Bryan and Sean. I told them that I was going to leave, and this treatment of Brian just confirmed it. Brian insisted that he had other offers on the table and told me not to be so silly but thanked me for the support anyway. I told him that my mind was made up and with or without him, I was going to start CCL, but he should start it with me. The other 2 were with me, they were as disgusted as I was about the treatment Brian received from the company and were ready to take the leap of faith and now it was just down to timelines and getting things done. Fate steps in again; When a popular member of staff leaves a thriving business, word gets around, especially around the airport.

By coincidence, the managing director of a local trucking company got wind of Brian leaving JAG and was interested in discussing with him to come into his business (Westbay) to do what he did at JAG for Westbay. Brian explained that he was now going into business with 3 other colleagues and declined the offer. The managing director Dave Williams reached out again and said that he liked that idea and that he was interested in investing in the startup. We had various meetings over the next few weeks, and it was decided that Dave would invest £40k into the business with a 60% stock shareholding and the rest of us would receive 10% each. Put it this way, £40k was a lot of money then and allowed us to set up properly as a business with the right equipment etc; so, without hesitation we accepted the deal and now the only thing holding us back was the paperwork.

We were all ready to go, on the eleventh hour, literally Sean decided to back out and never signed the agreement. I remember being at home in my 1-bedroom flat in Neasden NW London, getting ready to leave the house to sign the agreement documents when Brian called me and said that we had a problem. He said Sean's out, not sure about Bryan so what do you want to do? We looked at Sean as being the one that would keep everything ticking over. His knowledge was second to none, he was smart and knowledgeable and after all he came up with the name Customs Clearance Limited, the brand that went on to serve us for years.

Having Sean onboard would attract high end clientele, not going to lie, Sean not joining us was a massive blow but also a reality check, the grass isn't always greener on the other side. Bryan N was also a concern as he and Sean were brothers-in-law. Me and Brian K obviously thought that Bryan N would be out because of his affiliation with his brother-in-law. We were both wrong, Bryan N was in, he said the opportunity is too good to turn down "I'm in "he said. The 3 of us met up later that evening with Dave and signed the documents, CCL was born.

Established the 1st of April 1999… (That year, a huge year)
What a year.

JAG made it hard for me. Made it difficult for CCL to trade. They took me to court, said that I took company property and approaching clients which was deemed to be illegal. The company property that they said that I stole was my own knowledge that I copied yes onto company paper and yes, I filed into company folders, but the intelligence belonged to me, things that I learnt over the years, and it just made sense to me to store all that knowledge somewhere. Eventually I gave up and started a fresh intel log file. A lot of the knowledge was in my head so I more or less duplicated over time what I had had before and I still ahem that same file today, that has my name on it, and nobody can take away from me. I couldn't approach customers but customers could approach me so that was a tricky one, but it worked out fine in the end. They did everything they could to stop us from trading, they did everything. They were the disruptors of everything. I've said it before but you're going to hear me say it again, I had a lot going on in my life at that time. 1999 was a massive year for me. Looking back on it, it was huge.

Established the 1st of April 1999 – CCL's first official day, we are now open for business.
Both me and Bryan N were working out our notice and I was trying to get things in order to try and make the transition a lot smoother

than it actually was. J.A.G made life miserable in trying to stop me, especially from trading. They couldn't actually stop CCL from trading, but they could make life difficult for me, in which they did. I put this down to experience, managed the situation the best I could and moved on. I had other things to worry about, I had a business to run and although officially I couldn't work at CCL, in the background, I was pulling strings, reaching out to my network and trying to get the main things done and being ready for the onslaught of new business. As well as starting a new business in 99, me and Lesa were pregnant, we were expecting our first baby in and around august/ September time so not only did I have a business to run and needed that to work like pronto, but we were also planning a wedding in December and moving into a new home around May/ June.

You could say a few months ago I was living an easy life but now, only to put myself under so much pressure, did I have regrets, would I have regrets. I've asked myself that same question every day since and the answer has unanimously always been a swift NO! You see, the way I look at things, there's no such thing as a free lunch, you've probably heard that saying before? You reap what you sow, you put the work in, you will get the results, Rome wasn't built in a day – but it was built. Those first 3 to 4 years were a very turbulent time in and out of work, I knew I had a mental toughness, but this was much tougher than tough, this was a mental resilience. It wasn't easy, if it was supposed to beast, everybody would be doing it. They say in the first 3 years is the make or break for any business. You get through those 36 months, like likely hood of a sustainable business is over 50%. In our 1st 2 years we had some big issues, well they were big for us.

Within that 1st 12 months of the business my daughter Mya was born on June 8 weeks premature. We got the keys to our new home in and around the same time while Lesa and Mya were still in the hospital. Mya couldn't leave the hospital because she was so premature and so tiny. When Mya was born, she was only 1 pound 12 and she was so tiny she measured from head-to-toe approx. 8 inches. I know this because she would fit snuggly in the palm of my hand. Mya was in the incubation unit for premature babies until she was strong enough to come home. Lesa stayed for the 1st 4 weeks with her so you could imagine it was a testing time for us but we manifested through and battled on. The power of manifestation is incredible, we did what we had to do to make things happen. You see, at this point, I knew I had the mental resilience to conquer most things. This J.A.G disruption was nothing compared to real life or death situations, with lots of ups and downs, we remained positive as a family and that helped me to remain focused in business.

Lesa went into see her consultant at kings college hospital, Denmark Hill, London for a routine checkup and observation only to be told that they were rushing her into the maternity ward as the baby had stopped growing and they would have to perform a caesarean (c-section) immediately. I remember being at work in the office, not been there long, possibly around a few hours when I got the call from Lesa telling me that she was on her way to the maternity ward, and they are keeping her in and if I could get her an overnight bag. Of course, the conversation shocked me, but I listened and reacted in a way as not to panic, I didn't want to freak out the situation more than necessary.

Done a quick handover with Brian K and Bryan N then made a quick phone call to a good friend of mine Patrick who worked as a field engineer, his job was flexible and if he wasn't on a job, I knew I could count on him to drop me off near to a tube station so that I could be on my way and meet Lesa at the hospital. Patrick came to get me and said he would drop me at the hospital, desperate times, desperate measures he said and within the hour I was by Lesa's side offering comforting support at this very traumatic time. But we were calm, we always remained calm and positive throughout the time.

I didn't have a car; I didn't even have access to one at this time because the business wasn't really making any money. We were turning over but not making any profit as such. The plan was to take as much money as we needed, enough to cover rent or mortgage and living costs that we had so that the company had some breathing space to grow. Working with J.A.G, I was used to a certain lifestyle, didn't scrimp and scrape and definitely wasn't watching the pennies. Now, it was almost like taking steps backwards in order to move forward, it was more like taking a hundred steps backwards to move1 step forward. This is how I measured things at the time.

At J.A.G I had 4 company cars in all the time I was there. I drove a red rover convertible, Ford Sierra SE, Vauxhall Tigra and a Land Rover Freelander. The car that I handed back before leaving was the Land Rover Freelander, a 4 x 4 vehicle that I liked a lot so it kind of hurt me to have to give it back. This was my benchmark going forward. In order to get back to that starting line, the Freelander was the aim, my thought process was to aim for the Freelander and if the business did well, then it would be possible to achieve and if the business didn't do well then, who knows. The task was set, the plan was in action, work hard, earn, spend your money on something you desire enough and make it happen. Manifestation! It took me another 3 years before I could afford that Landrover Freelander, but purchased that Freelander and from there set myself of milestone bench marks that I went onto achieve.

As I mentioned, I didn't have a car so had to rely on public transport to get to work. Now living in Streatham South London and working at Heathrow west London, literally on the opposite side of town from each other. Luckily for me, living in a city like London, public transport was/ is relatively widespread where transportation runs frequently. I would leave the house on Ellison Road, walk to Streatham High Road, take the 109 bus to Brixton, take the Victoria line train to Green Park, change at Green Park, take the Piccadilly line to Heathrow. I would get off at Hatton Cross station or sometimes terminal 4, depending on what Brian K was doing. Put it this way. Brian had a vehicle, he was smart, he had a company car at J.A.G but never sold his burgundy ford Orion or was it an Escort so he had this vehicle to fall back on. This was now the official company run around.

Bryan N would make his own way to the office, his wife worked at British Airways and had a car and would drop him off in the mornings and he'd find a way home in the evenings. He didn't live that far away unlike me, so his journey was more manageable. We had a system. Brian K would be the first person in the office. He would be in at around 05:30 hrs and leave to go home by at least 3:00 pm if not earlier depending on what was going on. Over the years we perfected the schedule so that the early shift would finish at midday and go home. Our system, I would aim to arrive in the Heathrow area by no later than 10:30 am. Usually I would go to terminal 4, wait for Brian to pick me up either on his way to the bank or after doing the banking run in Hatton Cross across the road from the tube station.

That's what we did, every morning we had to do the bank run, paying in cash or cheques from the previous day. It worked a treat for the longest while. In the evening, I would stay in the office until close where I would lock up around 6 or 7 and get a lift back to terminal 3 where I would jump on the tube from David Shawn a friend of Bryan N that started his business in and around the same time we started ours and was renting space within our office. The system worked well Monday to Friday but on the weekend, Brian K had to cover both Saturday and Sunday mornings alone as he was the only one that had access to a vehicle then. This must have gone on for at least 6 months to a year until we were in a position to lease a vehicle for me. Those day you could lease a vehicle for as little as £150.00 per month inclusive of maintenance and insurance you just needed to look around for a good deal. At the time, all we could afford was £90.00 that we managed to push to £96.00 per month and we took on our first lease vehicle, a navy blue 3 door Vauxhall Corsa. The lease agreement was 3 years and even though the car wasn't my cup of tea, it served its purpose, I wasn't proud or embarrassed, it was a journey and the task at hand was to get the Landrover Freelander which was accomplished a few years later.

Meanwhile, sitting with the consultants at Kings going through the procedure of the c- section and what to expect, as I disappeared to change into my surgical clothing looking like an actual surgeon myself, I could hear Lesa discussing vitals with somebody that I came to know as the midwife. I've said this before, fate has a funny way of presenting itself in the least unexpected moments. As I came into the room the midwife looked up and stared me in the face. She said, "Are you Rudolph Bertie, do you remember me?" At that without hesitation I replied, "of course I remember you but what you are doing here, why aren't you at school" Kirsty was the younger sister of one of my old schools class mate Daniel Scott and she Was now the midwife that had the task and responsibly to deliver our baby. This was amazing how weird, instantly me and Lesa were put at ease as now we had someone that I knew personally that put us in the comfort zone but thinking back at that time, she must have been under so much pressure, not sure how long she was in the Job and how many babies she delivered but the occasion didn't seem to unnerve her, she went about her business diligently and helped to deliver our beautiful baby girl. The perfect situation, beautiful wife, beautiful baby, beautiful life, what else can a man ask for.

When Mya was born, a few days later I picked up the keys for our new home from the estate agent. Because Lesa was caring for Mya at the hospital, I had to organize the move all by myself. I didn't even have a car so how was I even going to attempt to do this? Where there's a will, there's always a way. At this point we were temporarily living in Lesa's rented accommodation on Knights Hill West Norwood just a short drive to the new property on Ellison Road but we had a lot of stuff to move, A couple months before, I sold my 1 bedroom flat in Neasden used the money from the sale of that flat to put down as a deposit on the new purchase. All my belongings were moved out and now taking up residents in Lesa's small little one bedroom.

One weekend, I organized to borrow a transit van from one of my suppliers. Sonny from Packages Express agreed that I could have the transit over the weekend at no cost, but I had to refuel it. I thought that was a good deal. I also had my friends, a few of them on hand to help me move from Lesa's flat into the new home. To make it more interesting, I offered Richie, Carty, Rhino and Reid, I think Hooligan was there too, drinks and dinner courtesy of Kentucky fried chicken (KFC) bargain bucket and without further ado, they all signed up to agree to help me on the weekend. That Friday after work, I went to the depot of Packages Express where I met Sam, Sonny's business partner. I was here for the transit it said, Sam looked at me and said, "what transit?" Puzzled I replied "the one Sonny reserved for me" he said "we don't have a spare transit, there all out but I have a 7 and a half tonne that you can have and I don't need it back until Tuesday – you do know how to drive a 7 and a half tonne don't you?" I gulp for a second and said, "yeah sure" not overly keen or confident to take it, what choice did I have, everything was lined up for the weekend and I had to move everything out of Lesa's flat into our new home that weekend because the council needs that property empty to move in a new family. The last time I actually drove a 7 and a half tonne vehicle was when I worked for FOB but that was just back and forward around the yard nothing major like on the motor way through busy London traffic, where the hell was, I even going to park the thing was all that was going through my head. Oh well, I'd better get on with it, I still need to visit Lesa and Mya in the hospital, so I thanked Sonny and set about my way.

Back to business, CCL was thriving, still not making shit loads of money but things were heading in the right direction. Put it this way and this is where you really test your nerves. The first month of trading, we didn't have any business coming through because we were still setting things up plus, me and Bryan N were still working out our notice from our previous employer. The first week when we joined Brian K in the office, we still had no business, but we were optimistic. The phone didn't ring, maybe there was a fault on the line, that happens sometimes on new connection. We tested the line, nothing wrong with the phone line. The phone didn't ring all week until Friday afternoon around 3pm, the phone rang, we all stopped in our tracks and looked at each other with excitement, could this be the moment, could this be our first customer, who was on the other end of the call? Eventually I picked up the phone, but it was the wrong number! How deflating.

That week, no business but we remained optimistic. The following week I started to shake a few branches and chewed up a few contacts. It's ironic and remarkable at the same time that the customers that you rely on as friend in the business, the ones that say they have your back and when push comes to shove turn their back on you are the same ones that expect the most but want to pay you less. What I'm trying to explain is the ones that I thought would come didn't, well at least not at first anyway, and the ones that you least expected to come did.

The ones that we expected to make the move didn't jump because they didn't want to be the fall guy, their words not mine. One said, imagine if we moved all our business to you and you went out of business, imagine how that would impact our business and friendship, good point I thought, but at least have the conversation. On the flip side of that, a customer who we didn't expect to make the change called the office one day and was quite upset that we didn't approach him to tell him that we had moved on. All he kept saying was that he used to call up our old company only to be told that Brian and Rudee no longer work here and when he asked well where they have gone, they were told with we don't know. He said I've been trying to find you for weeks and now I have you I want you to have all my business. The lesson there was never judge a book by its cover.

We would go from strength to strength, more and more clients would find us more or less through word-of-mouth referrals and as a business we kept on growing. The first time we made a profit, this day felt like hitting the jackpot, it was an amazing feeling. Although it wasn't a lot of money, it was a lot of money for us. We were favorable with the bank and took advantage of what they had to offer by way of a deferment account, overdraft facility and a few company credit cards. I've always said this, where there's money, there's problems. If you've come across the term "money is the route to all evil", you will understand what I'm talking about. Put it this way, I'm not going to go into all the details because it's long, the 3 of us became 2 because one of us was stealing from the company through credit card purchases. Let's just leave it there.

We still had Dave Williams as our silent majority shareholder. He was sitting at 60% so for every pound £ we made he took home £0.60 pence, me and Brian K now owned 20% each and that didn't sit well with us. Don't get me wrong, all respect is due to Dave for actually fronting up the money and believing in us in the first place. Yes, he stuck by us and helped us through the rough times. He often extended credit terms when we used his services, he helped us with the bank and other creditors, but this is business, I expected he could see it coming, we were now making some decent money and we simply had to buy him out. Again, I'm not getting into the details of the deal, but we managed to agree on terms and now me and Brian K were now proud owners, 100% – 50/50 between us, it felt sweet, and we now felt like real bosses. More money, more problems.

We were making money but not putting any money aside for tax, schoolboy error I know, we've never made money like this before so what was the point, it wouldn't be that much anyway. As it goes, we made Monet that year and was issued a hefty tax bill and we didn't have the reserves to cover the cost. This was an issue, because we'd been brushing this to the side and burying our heads in the sand to some extent, it finally caught up to us and the government were demanding payment. We had to pay; we had no choice.

Umbrellas on a rainy day, remember this term. Where do you go when you're looking for a loan, the bank, so off we trod to Barclays Bank asking them for a bank loan to cover our corporation tax debt. School boy error. The bank said that they didn't loan against any debts to the government and our bank manager Jackie Whitfield went onto say, "well, if the government don't bankrupt you, we will" Nice advise right. Banks will throw bucket loads of money at you when you don't need it but immediately as you fall into hard times and you need the bank's help, they are nowhere to be seen and want to wash their hands of you. "You'll never be offered an umbrella from a bank on a rainy day"

Cut a long story short, we dealt with the matter in hand, overcame that hurdle, and the rest is history.

We simply had an overtrading cash flow issue and as soon as that was highlighted and we rectified the situation, we moved forward and continued to develop the business and took it from strength to strength.

Growing at a nice steady pace, you could see that we had a healthy business that we were both proud of. My parents had never seen me in work mode, so I thought it was about time I introduced them to what I was doing and why it took up so much of my time. Being the proud parents that they are, my father used to often brag to his friends that his son was a businessman and he's making his own money. That always made me feel good and focused me to do better. Apparently, when I was a young kid, I used to tell my parents that one day I was going to be a millionaire. I never really thought about it like that, I wanted CCL to be a success, and everyone connected to it.

My father had different ideas. I remember the first time they both came to the office at The Mill in Stanwell Moore, even though it was a small office, they were both impressed to see where my focus was, I was working in an office and running my own business, my father always used to tell me not to take a job where I had to work outside or in a factory so for him to see me on my journey to achieve my goals was an extremely proud moment for them both. I was the boss and had people working for me, he said and asked curiously "boy – you mek yuh fus million yet? "(boy, have you made your first millions yet?) Ashe laughed through his smile and I replied "still working on it, not yet, still trying" we all laughed then the conversation turned into, my first pair of trainers that I bought with my paper round money and all the luxury cars that I wanted to buy.. those days man, the good old days. Shortly after in 2001, I lost my father to Cancer, he was only 60. His dream was to return to St.kitts with my mother after retirement and to live happily ever after. That never happened unfortunately.

I remember, even on his death bed my father would always ask me if I'd made those millions yet and my answer would more or less be the same "not yet, nearly, still working on it" I knew he would discuss this with his friends because one of his good friends Eustace Herbert would often ask me randomly "boy – yuh mek yuh fus million yet" and we would laugh together but I wouldn't actually give an answer, I concentrated more on the sentiment, the force behind the drive that has carved out the journey to success.

CCL started off in an old water mill converted into serviced office, on the flight ✈ path, backing onto the main road that separates terminal 5 and the runway. However, the mill was there for a lot longer than terminal 5, I would imagine going back to the turn of the century. Believe it or not, the mill is famous for a British film that was made back in the day 1953 called Genevieve about Two veteran cars and their crews are participating in the annual London to Brighton Veteran Car Run. https://en.wikipedia.org/wiki/Genevieve_(film)

Reelstreets | Genevieve
"When Genevieve overheats, Wendy goes to fetch water. In front of The Mill House next to Stanwell Mill on Horton Road, Stanwell Moor, Middlesex."

Don't ask me why I remember this, but I do. The mill is a very historical listed building, apparently it was haunted, but that's not why we left the building. It wasn't a purposely built building for what we needed. We needed to have a warehouse, more space and a larger capacity to grow our business and expand on services. As much as we didn't want to leave the mill because it was a nice start up office, we outgrew the building and had to move somewhere much bigger.

Moving to Isleworth.
This was a game changer, and I remember it like yesterday. It was huge in comparison to where we just came from. I remember in the transition period I was responsible with all the logistics, setting up the comms, moving furniture and office equipment, ensuring the warehouse was adequate to take on the volume of new business we were expecting and most and overall ensuring that the building was security tight and secure.

One morning waiting for the telephone lines to be connected with no furniture in the building, I remember sitting on a packed out A4 size stationery box filled with photo copier paper. As the minutes turned into hours, still waiting, all I kept on thinking was how the hell I was going to stack this place out. How on earth was I going to fill the warehouse with cargo. That was the one thought that I had that bugged and troubled me for a while until we eventually moved in fully the following week and all of the freight that we had stored in other neighboring warehouses already superseded our own warehouse space, problem solved but now I'm faced with another problem, yep, need more space ... wow! The step up in size and cost to move into this new facility was gigantic, especially when as a business you're still growing and although we had now been established for 5 years, we were still in what I call the growing stages, so moving into this building was a big deal. We had internal discussions and decided in the end to take the leap of faith.

I must add, this was only made possible due to one solidifying fact. That fact was Mark Adams. Mark was one half of the world-famous courier company now known as Marken Limited, remember the company I went to and left very shortly after starting because invest there was no room for promotion, well Mark was the CEO there and he was the one that called and tried to change my mind to stay. We stayed in contact over the years and when I mentioned that we were looking for bigger premises with warehouse space, he said "why don't you buy mine, in Isleworth, St John's Road the old market building." I said "Buy – I can't afford to buy your building and by the way, which one, you have 3?"

He replied: "any one you want" and laughed. I expressed I was grateful for the offer, but I really wasn't in any position to buy any commercial property, which he insisted, yes you, he said "where there's a will there's a way" and continued to add that he would rent a property of my choice to us at market rate until we were in a comfortable position to purchase. Even if it took 5 years, he said that he was in a position to wait and that they were in no hurry to sell but they wanted to offload at some stage. The uniqueness of the name Marken is that it's a combination of the 2 founders, Mark Adams and Ken Powell, always fondly known as Mark and Ken, get the picture. Hello // We go beyond to connect patients with new medicines. Marken is now a UPS owned company specializing in pharmaceutical logistics.

We stayed in that facility in Isleworth for a good number of years. 2007 to 2016, managing to purchase one of the facilities and renting 2 of the neighbouring units, it was time to move on again why, because we outgrow the space again and business was suffering.

A lot of changes during our time there, had some really good staff in Anj & Dale that kept everything operational ticking over nicely then we went for a big sales drive and employed Neo. Neo was single handedly responsible for CCL' growth in China, he went out and won the business and Anj and her team managed the business and serviced the customers well. Having Anj and Neo on your team was like having an additional left and right hand. We had a good team; we had a strong team and me and Brian often complemented the team as we were truly blessed to have such a dedicated team around us. Making a difference makes all the difference and that's what we had in abundance in the staff that we had around us. You could see they felt part of it, I often referred to those times as "part of the CCL experience"

Networking and being in touch with the freight forwarding / cargo/ supply chain logistics community is a key component to the success of any business within our field. In order to stay ahead of the competition and introduce our business on a global platform, it made sense to join freight networks and industry associations alike.

We captured the imagination and the mood of the industry on a global landscape when we declared to the world that we were the "market leaders in eCommerce gateway customs clearance", testing the mood and pushing boundaries while feeding the appetite of this new revolutionary phenomenon in eCommerce. You see, we were actually managing eCommerce products and offering eCommerce solutions way before we heard the term eCommerce.

It was just freight management albeit freight management with a bespoke edge. The first big breakthrough with the eCommerce brand was working with DHLe (DHL eCommerce), formerly known as DHL global mail. Glen ford was the mastermind that engineered the deal when he approached me and Brian early on in the evening at a well-known bar in Dubai. If you know, you know… 😁 Being in Dubai in May was the industry "WMX" highlight event not to be missed. Everybody who was anybody involved in the distribution management of mail and parcels would be in attendance and this was the one annual event that we never missed. The approach went something like this, "I've been told that you guys can help me, I don't know what it is because I've never come across it before, but something has landed on my desk, they call it eCommerce and to tell the truth I don't have a clue."

I told him not to worry and that he'd come to the right people in the right place at the right time. The rest as they say is history. I'm putting this on record and taking some of the credit for DHLe's success. Having DHLe as a client opened many doors for us, the industry would monitor the success of DHLe, especially USA/ EU routings and wanted the same level of service that DHLe were getting. Our business took off again and it came with another level of challenges.

One of these challenges meant that we had to move into a much larger purpose-built facility or risk losing out on some major contracts so we were on the hunt for that next level facility which I knew would definitely take the business to peak levels as we continued to design and embed our DNA on the world circuit.

Just before moving in 2016, we were embroiled in a legal dispute that started in 2014 that took us all the way into 2015. At the same time, we negotiated and agreed to sell 20% shares to the Lenton Group a DPD Group/ GeoPost company. The legal issue disrupted and almost derailed the deal, it was something we wanted to happen and something we needed to do to strengthen our position in the market and remain steps ahead of the competition. It was a very sensitive frustrating time, testing, time consuming, stressful, we persevered through the turmoil and got the deal done.

It felt good to have to have some real money sitting on my bank balance, but it didn't last for long. That payment was enough to take care of some outstanding bills and pay off some of the mortgage, but it definitely didn't make us millionaires. At that moment I could hear my dad's voice "boy – yuh Mek yuh fus millions yet?", I smiled to myself and for the first time in my life, I started to believe it could happen. You always have doubts when you go into business, big dreams, big ambitions to start off with but along the way when things don't always go according to plan, that's when the doubt kicked in. This was different, I couldn't now see the path to financial freedom, the goal ahead was clear, it was a nice feeling and encouraged me to do more and to do better and encourage the people around me to do more and to do better.

If you want to be known as the best, you have to be seen as the best. Moving into radius park Hatton Cross was no mean feat, it took a lot of organization, coordination and communication oh and we underestimated the cost of the move and over budget by a lot. School boy error, but we made it work. Anj and Stu had the task of making it work, all I had to do was sign the cheques and move in. This move caused some rifts between me and Brian, nothing too serious that I couldn't deal with but there were obvious questions marks surrounding the move especially highlighting the spend. It was a big step up, a massive step up, a huge step up but looking at the bigger picture, it was a must have, it was a sacrifice and a gamble worth taking. I had no doubt in my mind whatsoever this was the right move for us if we were to be taking it seriously on the global stage.

We marketed well, our sales team was thriving and pushing

performance levels and now we had the building and facility that looked the part and something that we could stand in front of and call it CCL HQ. I remember a few years before when HM Customs paid us a visit to our Isleworth site. The first thing that was put to me was that they were expecting to see a much bigger building with a lot more personal. I said why would you think that and one of them said that our website portrayed that image. I smiled and said, "perception is in the marketing" She asked: "don't you think it's a bit misleading?" I replied "no, it worked for you didn't it" I don't think my comment went down too well.

2016/17 was a mad financial year for us, we were still paying off for the move, but numbers were up, and the warehouse was full. I remember when I viewed the building before moving in, I stood in the middle of the warehouse and thought how the hell am I going to fill this, a regular theme right... but we did. We were now managing and processing through our facility 30 to 40 million parcels per annum, year on year, this was obviously phenomenal, and we were doing well.

That dream had now become a reality, we were on the map as a leading brand in supply chain eCommerce logistics and it was the proudest feeling ever to be the architect of my own success, anything else on top would only be a bonus. Remembering all the struggles and pains we put ourselves through to get to this point, I specifically remember when both me and Brian signed a cheque for each other of £100k each and walking into the bank to deposit the cheque almost feeling as if we were doing something illegal. We earned it, we could afford it, so we deserved it.

On another occasion when I attended a WCA conference in Hong Kong at the regal hotel. The hotel that joins the airport, this was the first event that I attended, and all my business cards were done on the first day, at the cocktail reception. At this event, I was sitting in the piano lounge when a guy that I previously met asked me if I was running my own business or if my business was running me. I felt quite offended at the time and asked him why he would say that, after all I had introduced myself as the CEO so obviously, I was running my own business.

He said: "well – I can't help noticing you keep looking at your mobile phone, I assume your checking your email"

He was correct, I was in fact looking at my emails and checking back with the office.

He said: "can the office run without you being there?"

Taken back I replied: "sure it can"

He carried on, "so why check your messages then, why now, why not later when your out of site back in your hotel room?"

He made a valid point and something that has stuck with me forever and as soon as I got back to London, I put measures in place to ensure I was only contacted and expected to react on my travels if something was extremely urgent and needed my full attention. Anything else would have to wait until I got back. So, thanks Richard Thornton, that piece of advice definitely helped to shape the person that I am today.

From those early days way back in 1999 we took our chances and as they say, the rest is history. My story is all about ambition and determination and not settling for anything less than what you deserve.

We never wanted to become a large corporation, but we ended up being part of a conglomerate organization, we only intended to employ around 10 people or so but ended up with 60 plus if not more.

Any business that I started was purely for the purpose of improving or to be alternative. The motto, "do better" I think we definitely achieved that. We set out to improve our financial situation and that we did and then some.

Brian left the business in 2018 after selling the remainder of his shares to the Lenton group. Italian got to the point that we were no longer the majority party, and he simply lost the appetite. Mark Adams once said to me, "the moment you lose the ability to sign your own cheques, that's the moment to cash in." This was the case for Brian.

We had a good innings, now I'm the last man standing. From those lunch conversations in 1998 with the four of us, to actually creating a business, making a decent living from it and employing other people who would be reliant on the business, from the original 4, I was the last man standing but I wasn't ready to hang up my boots yet, I still had a lot of energy, enthusiasm and was ready to go again.

I'm a big admirer of footwear, especially trainers I have my fair share, my wife says I have a problem. As much as I explain my story and as much as she can relate, she still says I have a problem. All I say is she's lucky I don't have my fair share of luxury cars...

Life's goals change as we grow. What was important yesterday may not be so important today. Now the last man standing and staying on as the CEO, I would encourage the people around me to do better, to achieve the maximum they could ever dream of achieving, push the boundaries and don't be afraid of criticism and be open to change. I took an interest in mentoring, developing the under privileged and sponsoring up and coming athletes and investing in startup businesses. I'm a big advocate of giving back to the community and supporting the next generation with as much knowledge, guidance and support as it needs from me.

Amongst all the upheaval and fiasco of Brexit and the disasters of the pandemic, those last few years between 2018 and 2022 were probably the greatest financial years of CCL. It was important to me to oversee the business through Brexit and to steer it through the pandemic, remain as the market leader and leave the business on a high in healthy financial shape but most importantly in good hands.

The last man standing has now left the building. As I sit back and reflect over the last 3 decades, I feel a sense of accomplishment and achievement and listen to my father's word; "boy – yuh Mek yuh fus millions yet?"

So, what am I doing now? After leaving CCL, I never wanted to compete against them, to compete against CCL would be like raising a family, turning your back on your kids and starting a new family. That wouldn't sit right with me. For a while I concentrated on a few interesting projects, guiding and advising technology companies looking to access the logistics space but now I'm heavily focused on my own brand projects that complement each other, (Nonexe, Nex, ATem Group and iDX)taking all my experience into this space remaining creative, flexible and neutral, testing the waters, open to change, still pushing boundaries, still wearing hoodies with an alternative outlook. There's always another way.

Apply yourself and achieve the most!!

The end.

Rudee, Bertie
Visionary Leader in eCommerce Logistics

Rudee is a specialist in cross-border supply chain eCommerce logistics. He has spent his entire career within cross-border, **founding Customs Clearance Ltd (CCL) in 1999** and spearheading the company through **23 years of development, expansion and innovation**. Under Rudee's leadership, **CCL has earned a global reputation as the benchmark in service excellence.**

Personal and Commercial Methodology
Rudee is a communicator, a **strategic thinker** and **problem-solver**, an acknowledged **innovator and thought feeder**. He is available to guide and assist individuals and businesses alike to **think creatively and plan rigorously**. He advises and mentors on a wide range of issues facing **leadership, growth strategy** & **change management**.

Today Rudee continues to be **entrepreneurial with that creative spirit** offering **guidance and support in mentorship**, encouraging the next generations leaders.

Current position(s):

- Founder – Nonexe Limited.
- Co-founder & Chairman – NeX Limited.
- Co-founder & Chairman – ATeM Group.

When Rudee's not working, he likes to chill and relax especially at home with his beautiful wife **Lesa** and daughter **Mya** and also spending quality time with extended family and friends"
 – There's no place like home –

Reach out to Rudee: linkedin.com/in/rudeebertie

Chapter 3

Mandy Deakin-Snell

My story

Sometimes, events happen in your life that are quite unexpected and serendipitous.

Before discovering the world of supply chain, I didn't know what I wanted to do. I was driven by a burning desire to create a better life than the one I knew. The worry of what to do after leaving school weighed heavily on me, and having no one to confide in left me feeling lost and uncertain about the future. The one thing I did know was that I needed a job to earn money and help my mom, who was struggling to raise our family on her own.

As the eldest of three children, I had to play the role of an adult and step up to support the family financially and emotionally, to make up for what we had lost after my dad left us when I was 13. With a seven-year gap between my brother and me, and being nine years older than my sister, there was an expectation to mind my siblings and help around the house while mom went back to working full time to put food on the table.

It was a tough time for all of us, but it was a time when I developed resilience and resourcefulness, which has served me well over the years.

Leaving school at nearly seventeen, I landed what would now be called an apprenticeship with a prestigious blue-chip company, working in their IT administration department at their head office. Back then, computers were huge.

I can still feel the nervous excitement as I approached the massive double doors of what they called the "computer room." My heart raced as I waited for someone to let me in with a security pass. When the doors finally opened, a blast of icy air rushed out, revealing a room unlike anything I had ever imagined. Towering six-foot-high glass cabinets filled with blinking, multi-coloured lights, humming electronic equipment, and the slow rotation of large round spools of tape processing endless streams of data were mesmerising. In that moment, I realised there was so much more to big companies than letters and filing!

This was the start of my corporate journey, and I loved being part of a huge organisation. It felt safe and secure, and being surrounded by smart people who were willing to teach and encourage me meant every day was a new opportunity to learn and grow. It was exciting to see where this new path would lead.

The company eventually took me on permanently and supported me with time off to go to college and qualify in business studies. Working in different departments meant I got to learn all aspects of business administration and corporate contracts. It was still an emotional roller coaster at home but immersing myself in martial arts was something that got me out of the house, and a where I learned to appreciate the power of the mind, body connection.

Looking back, the immersive training and supportive colleagues were crucial in helping me navigate some very tough times in my late teens. Mental well-being wasn't something that was openly discussed at work back then, but this is what I learned:

The combination of physical activity, immersive learning and supportive mentors helps enormously, and something I encourage you to embrace. Finding someone you trust, who is wise and supportive is priceless.

Things weren't going well at home, so at the age of 18 I left. Finding somewhere to live with a low income wasn't easy but luckily, I found shared accommodation in a large house with five students. It was an interesting time, and great being part of their world even though I didn't get to go to university. I had left home with very little so was incredibly grateful when my work colleagues rallied round to collect homeware for me. My little room was downstairs next to the kitchen, so I had very little sleep as there was always someone running a tap or boiling a kettle. But it was a place to stay for now.

Work was going well, and I earned a few promotions, allowing me to save money for first time in my life. It was a new chapter and after moving several times I ended up staying briefly with my estranged father whilst deciding my next move. But things took a turn for the worse when he was diagnosed with cancer, and I ended up staying longer than expected to help take care of him during chemotherapy. One day, I came home to find him severely dehydrated and near death. I called an ambulance to get him to hospital urgently. He was furious, insisting that he wanted to die and threatened me as he was being taken off on a stretcher. He survived.

After that episode, he vowed that cancer would never beat him, saying that the only time he would give up again is if he couldn't drive.

He went on to fight various cancers for fifteen years after that, I never met anyone with his determination and strength of mind. The week he had to stop driving because his legs were so swollen from the treatment after having his stomach removed, was the week he passed away.

The only advice my father ever gave me was to buy my own home instead of the sports car I wanted. I had a gut feeling he was right, and it was time to settle down and buy a place of my own. As luck would have it, I found a house near the city centre on a bus route to work. It was an urgent sale, so the lower price was just within reach. I stretched my finances, borrowing as much as possible and cashed in savings to make it happen.

I realise how fortunate I was to own my own home at 22 years of age when nowadays many young people don't get the chance with the higher cost of living and spiralling house prices. It was a blessed relief to not have to keep moving, but the reality was that whilst my full-time job meant I could pay the mortgage and bills, there was nothing left for food and a life outside of work. This meant taking two additional jobs to make up the shortfall of money. I found a bar job for three nights a week and joined an insurance company, knocking on doors for them two evenings a week to generate leads.

I was never afraid of hard work and had a steely determination to keep my precious new home. However, a year later, having three jobs took its toll on my immune system. It was so low that I contracted food poisoning and after three weeks of suffering, I was rushed to hospital, severely dehydrated and diagnosed with something more serious.

It's amazing what a week in hospital can do for self-reflection. As I lay hooked up to a drip in an isolation ward, staring at the ceiling and feeling sorry for myself, I started to think about my life more seriously. After martial arts I had taken up aerobics and circuit training, it kept my mind occupied and body in shape but having three jobs just wasn't sustainable anymore. If I wanted to stay healthy and keep my home, I needed to earn more money. When I got out of hospital, I decided to look for a better paying job.

A friend of mine at the time was working in sales, and not only did she get paid well, but she also drove a very nice white sports car. So, I decided that my next job would be in sales, despite having no experience, I believed I could learn fast and do it. She kindly arranged an interview for me with her boss. Although I lacked the sales experience they needed and they didn't offer any entry level sales training, her boss was encouraging. He told me I had great potential and assured me that if I found a role with basic sales training, after six months, he would offer me a job.

That was it… I was on a mission to find any sales job with training and a company car, and contacted numerous companies, finally managing to get an interview with a business near to where I was living. The interview was tough and through sheer determination and overcoming all their objections as to why they should give me the job when I had no sales experience, something must have convinced them as they agreed to take me on. Voila! My very first sales job was going to be selling vending machines for hot and cold drinks, with no experience in sales whatsoever!

I remember feeling positive and enthusiastic and the Managing Director who interviewed me picked up on my energy and said I came across authentic, with self-belief and determination, and because of this he was willing to give me a chance. This was a huge turning point in my life, and I never looked back. Little did I know then that this would lead down a path to my lifelong career in supply chain!

Finding a new career path in something I'd never done before taught me a valuable lesson that I used many times over the years, and one that may help you:

When you make up your mind to do something positive your

energy changes for the better and people pick up on this. What you project to others is unspoken, and enables you attract positive outcomes.

My first day in the new job was, to put it mildly, eye-opening. The sales manager I reported to was abrupt. He threw me a set of car keys and an A-Z map of Birmingham then told me my car was outside and my sales territory was in the map, and to get out there and sell some machines! Stunned, I asked about sales training. He mentioned that training would be in their London offices in two weeks. That was fine, but I was completely lost on where to start. When I politely asked for help, the conversation turned awkward, especially when I found out from the sales team that he didn't believe women could sell. Despite his impatience, he grudgingly agreed to let me spend a week on the road with him. He ended the conversation off by saying that I wouldn't last long anyway. "Really?" I thought. We'll see about that!

To be fair, as rude as he was with me on my first day, he turned out to be one of the most generous people I had ever met and a great mentor. He was the best salesperson in the company and prided himself on selling the most vending machines anyone had ever sold. That first week on the road together made him realise that not only was I serious about succeeding in sales (I was still thinking of that sports car with the other company) he also realised I had determination, a great work ethic and plenty of resilience to ignore his bad manners and foul language.

He taught me everything he knew about sales, although I'm not sure his direct approach would be acceptable these days, but back then it seemed to work. It was the hard knock school for selling, that's for sure.

The week before the official sales training course in London, I was sent out on the road on my own to do some cold calling. I was told that my only objective was to knock on as many doors as possible and get leads to book a vending machine demonstration. I was reminded to only book companies that had 12 staff or more, otherwise the cost would be too high, and we couldn't compete against a kettle!

Driving to a town called Oldbury near Birmingham city centre, I pulled into a car park and sat there with my heart racing, wondering where to start. Ironically, the second supply chain company where I would spend 21 years of my career was only half a mile from that carpark. Who knew?!

I can't recall how many office and factory doors I knocked that day, but it was a lot! Some people were kind, and some weren't. At one company a man escorted me out of their reception by my shoulder pads when I kept asking why they wouldn't book a demonstration with free coffee when they had more than enough staff to justify a machine. I was undeterred. In fact, being told I couldn't do something made me more determined and became a helpful belief pattern throughout my career

Eventually, I found a company who agreed to a demo. It was a proud moment back at the office announcing I'd booked my first demonstration for the following day. After much grilling about who they were, I reluctantly mentioned it was an engineering company with six staff. The team ridiculed me and said it was a waste of time because they didn't need a drinks machine and probably had nowhere to put it. They were right. When I did my very first demo, I had to balance a big desktop machine on the side of a ceramic sink. As I tried to demonstrate how delicious the drinks were, all the nozzles got blocked up from the taps that splashed water when people needed to wash their hands, and the machine failed to work. No-one got to taste the special coffee or delicious hot chocolate I tried to make for them. What a disaster!

The following week in London for the sales training course I felt hopeful as this would get me the training needed for the other job with the better car. At that time, I was driving a basic Ford Escort and couldn't wait to give it back. There were twelve of us on the course and I was the only woman, which was a usual trend throughout my career, especially in the male dominated supply chain sector later on.

On the second day of the course, the group was lively, and we were all chatting about the MD that had interviewed me when he suddenly he walked in. The room went quiet as he made an announcement that one of us had already sold their first machine. There was a lot of excited whispers as the guys in the group got more and more competitive saying they knew it must be them. Well, I knew it wasn't me. I blew the only chance of getting my first sales order when I couldn't make anyone a drink to sample whilst balancing my demo machine with blocked-up nozzles on the side of a ceramic sink!

"I'm pleased to say" the MD continued, "it's our very first female salesperson, Mandy, well done!" He started clapping and everyone followed his lead as they looked at me in disbelief. I was in shock and started questioning if it was true as surely it couldn't have been that little engineering company in Oldbury. It was.

Against all the odds, I had made my first sale. The only thing I could imagine had happened was that my boss had told them I would be fired if I didn't get the sale, and they just felt sorry for me. Either way, it was the first of many sales and that year I won one of their top prizes for highest sales in the company and the only female salesperson to achieve it. Tenacity, resilience and all my efforts were starting to pay off.

I never did join that other company after my sales training, mainly because I was earning good money by doubling my salary with commission, plus, I was having so much fun working with an amazing bunch of people, having a great boss who looked out for me, and receiving appreciation and recognition from the MD for all the money

I was bringing in for the company. It was an intoxicating combination and something I craved for the rest of my career.

It was a sad day when the company got taken over by a big conglomerate. One of their directors interviewed me and asked what I thought they should do with the company. I was astounded that he expected a 23-year-old to know the answer and felt they should be telling me the company strategy and why it would be of benefit to stay with them. Feeling disillusioned I called a recruitment agency in the city to help me find my next job with no preference for what that would be, just how much I wanted to earn and what car I wanted to drive.

That same weekend, I was staying at my aunt and uncle's house, and I mentioned about needing another job. My uncle suggested contacting the company he worked for as they were always looking for good salespeople. At the time, he was a driver for TNT Express UK and was proud to work for them. However, I had no aspirations to sell parcels so smiled politely and said I would think about it.

On the Monday after my weekend with my aunt and uncle, I had an interview with the agency. They had three jobs they thought would be suitable. The first one was for a cleaning company selling their services which I said no to. The next one was a job with TNT Express selling their domestic parcel service. I couldn't tell you what the third job was because I was too busy laughing about the coincidence of them offering me to go for an interview with the company my uncle had been promoting all weekend.

> At this point it's worth mentioning that whenever serendipity shows up, I follow my gut instinct, it has never let me down. Learning to trust your instinct about something or someone will pay off in the long run.

After researching the company and discovering they transported horses in their QT 146 'Quiet Trader' aircraft, I was hooked. Who knew supply chain could be so diverse; this could be more interesting than I expected. There were two interviews for the job, one with the sales Manager and one with the General Manager, both of whom were interesting, intelligent and believed in women salespeople. This gave me faith that this would be a good place to work. I was offered the job and whilst I didn't get the car of my dreams, the Volkswagen Jetta was fast, and the basic salary was better.

This is the moment where I stepped outside my comfort zone and entered the supply chain industry to sell a service instead of a product and where a whole new world opened up for me. I never looked back.

The lessons learned:

- Be open to opportunities even if they present themselves in peculiar ways
- Do your research and be curious about the company when applying for a job
- Be prepared to step outside your comfort zone to try something new, you never know where it might take you!

Those first few weeks at TNT selling their express parcel service seemed too easy compared to what I had been doing before. Selling expensive machines and signing companies up for five and ten-year contracts was a tough sell. The service industry was different. At that time, it was a yes or no to use your service and I left calls with fingers crossed hoping that they would.

It didn't take me long to get despondent. There was a feeling of not achieving much and potentially losing my job. This created anxiety as I still had my house to pay for and there was no-one to back me up if this went horribly wrong. After raising my concerns with the sales manager, he sat me down with what was then called a 13-week roller (basically a huge computer printout tracking all the sales I had made) to show me how well I was doing. Relieved, I continued selling and checking the printout for results. At that point I had no ambition to be a manager or climb the corporate ladder.

That was until I saw *the* shoes...

During an admin day, a woman I hadn't seen before walked into the office. She looked so elegant and professional and wore what appeared to be very expensive shoes. In fact, they were the most beautiful shoes I had ever seen! I can see them now, brown suede with a little bow on the back and small gold studs around the heels. I wondered what job she did in this company to afford shoes like those. It reminded me of how motivated I was to own more than the one pair I had when I was little and telling my mom I would buy lots of expensive shoes when I grew up.

I found out the amazing shoes belonged to the Regional Sales Manager. It was in that very moment I decided (without knowing anything about the role) that I wanted that job. A job that would enable me to afford to buy expensive shoes. It became my motivation for climbing the corporate ladder and that's why I applied to be a sales Manager at my first opportunity.

It may seem like a shallow motivation but having come from a background where we had very little money, expensive shoes was a luxury I could only dream of. Seeing someone who had achieved my dream was inspiring and rekindled my desire to achieve more...

> Find whatever it is that motivates you in life, something that grabs your attention and gets you out of your comfort zone to moves you forward, even if it is a pair of expensive shoes!

When my boss was promoted, I applied right away for his position. Having won 'Best Newcomer of the Year' and smashing all my targets, I believed I'd get the promotion. However, the General Manager thought I was too new and too young to take the role, plus there was a more mature person after it who was considered to have more experience. Despite providing a compelling argument as to why I was the best person for the role, it wasn't enough. Yet something happened to make them decide to give us both the same role to see who did it best over the first twelve months. It was a poor decision. Needless to say, it didn't work and was confusing for the team.

It was during this time of competing for the role in management that I was head hunted by a competitor to join them as their sales manager. It was more money a better car and the position I wanted to get me closer to being regional sales manager and those expensive shoes. I took the job. Six months later, I realised I'd made a huge mistake. Somehow, the General Manager at TNT found out I was looking to leave their competitor and asked me to rejoin them in the sales managers role I had left because the other person hadn't worked out. I politely refused and as didn't believe in going back, only forward. He was persistent and called me with surprising news that their international division in London were keen to meet me and were prepared to put me on a flight to London to be interviewed by their senior management team. Of course, I didn't hesitate to say yes to a free flight! I'd only ever been on a plane once before and began to feel the enthusiasm of potentially working for the international division of TNT.

At the TNT Skypak offices, all the people that interviewed me were really encouraging and believed I had potential, especially after seeing my sales record. By the time the UK Country Manager interviewed me at the end of the day, his team had fed back that I was somebody worth investing in. He put me through my paces asking direct questions and testing my knowledge. There was something about the international division of TNT that sparked my curiosity, and I really wanted to get into this amazing division and said I'd be prepared to take a role as a sales executive and work my way up again, he refused and said based on my experience, sales management was the right position.

He asked me to wait and promptly left the room. When he came back, he announced that their only vacancy for a sales manager role was in Bristol, but believed it was too far away from where I lived. Jumping in quickly I said a commute was doable and I would also consider moving. I had no intention of losing this opportunity and was fortunate enough to have an interview arranged for me with the Regional General Manager of the Southwest. Before long, the Sales Manager's role in Bristol Depot was offered to me and a new journey began. My passion for international supply chain grew and flourished into something I never could have imagined.

The territory across the southwest of the UK was huge and I worked long hours to lead and develop my team, as well as having to achieve my own sales targets. We were doing well, and I loved having a team of my own and helping them progress by supporting them on joint sales visits.

It was during a day out visiting customers with one of the team that I had a sudden urge to learn a language. No idea where it came from, unless it was a premonition that I would work for a French company one day. Which I did! We were in a small village in Somerset buying a sandwich when I asked the shop assistant where I could buy some language tapes…yes, we had tapes back then, no instant gratification streaming for us! She said there was a WH Smith at the end of the High Street that might have what I was looking for. The sales guy thought I was nuts as this was just a little market town and couldn't imagine them selling language tapes. But as luck could have it, they did.

As I reached over to pick up Learning French is Easy (or something like that) a book on the shelf above nearly jumped out and knocked me on the head, metaphorically speaking. It was called 'The Power of Your Subconscious Mind' by Dr. Joseph Murphy. There was something about the title and the summary on the back that intrigued me. At the checkout paying for the book, I completely forgot about learning a new language. Another gut reaction that led me on a whole new trajectory to study the power of the mind and discover how our words and thoughts control our behaviours and ultimately our outcomes. More on that later.

Working long hours, driving over 160 miles commuting to and from work every day on top of driving across my territory was tiring. I hadn't moved home because of my husband's job at the time and as much as I loved what I did, it was clear it was no longer sustainable. Late one evening, driving home on the motorway in the dark, rain pouring down, tired from a long day, I started to doze off. Then suddenly, jolted awake just as I was about to drive into the back of a lorry. I braked with a skid and managed to pull over to the side of the motorway, still in shock knowing that if I hadn't suddenly woken up in time, I would certainly have hit the lorry in front of me. When I eventually arrived home shaken and upset, my beloved husband, Keith, insisted that it was no longer safe for me to commute, and it was time to look for a job nearer home. The next day I contacted my boss to tell him the bad news.

No job is worth killing yourself for and if you're a work acholic like I was, don't wait for something like this to make you realise that your health is non-negotiable, as no amount of money will replace your well-being.

The company were amazing when I told them and they insisted they would help me find something else and fortunately, a few weeks later, a position came up nearer to home in their Birmingham branch.

I joined the depot as their new international sales manager and went on to become the Area Sales Manager. We got off to a great start and won top performing sales team of the year. It started to get me noticed and one day whilst out on the road with the Regional Director, he asked what I would like to do next. My thoughts went back to those beautiful suede shoes and without skipping a beat I said, Regional Sales Manager. Although the company had removed the role during a cost cutting exercise the previous year, he believed they may re-instate it. Well, they did. I applied and eventually got the promotion into my dream job.

Manifested to perfection, I walked through the office in my first pair of expensive shoes. They weren't brown suede, but they were beautiful! Proof that you can get anything you put your mind to. I encourage you to keep dreaming, keep believing and keep working towards your goals and dreams and don't let anyone tell you it can't be done. It doesn't have to be materialistic goals, just something that makes your heart sing loud enough to take gut action.

Back in the late eighties and nineties TNT was recognised as being one of the best delivery companies in the UK and prided itself on training staff in every aspect of leadership and supply chain. Under the formidable leadership of Alan Jones OBE, the company thrived for many years. He instilled in us the ethic of developing people and putting the customer first, and no matter what position you held in the company, everybody had to pick up the phone within three rings. This positive approach to training people to give them the best chance of success and putting the customer first, stayed with me throughout my career and served me well.

During one of these training courses, my life was about to take another new direction. That day there was a buzz in the air about a newly available general management position in East Midlands depot. Someone asked if I planned to apply and soon, others joined in encouraging me go for it. But I wasn't interested, I loved being a regional sales manager and had never aspired to be a general manager. That was until a voice called out "you couldn't do it anyway." I looked over to see one of the guys on the course muttering that I could never be a general manager. For some reason, although applying for the job hadn't entered my head, I felt triggered in a way I couldn't explain.

After discussing the role with my husband, he encouraged me to go for it. The next day I handed my boss an envelope, he looked horrified and told me I couldn't resign. After explaining that it wasn't a resignation letter, just my application for the role in East Midlands, he reminded me that I was succeeding in the job of my dreams and never wanted to be a General Manager. "Well, I do now." I said, and he smiled asking who had told me I couldn't do it, knowing only too well that when someone said I couldn't do something I would go out of my way to prove them wrong.

After a brief conversation and handing the envelope back that I was trying to give him, he eventually said he wasn't going to put me forward for the promotion and that I would need to apply directly to the country manager. It was disappointing to hear, especially after all my hard work and the success for his depot. To be honest, this was just one of many times someone tried to hold me back and failed. When I felt something was right, I followed my gut, and nothing could stop me.

It was during an event when all the senior managers got together that my male colleagues insisted that I speak to the country manager about my application. I was reluctant and said it wasn't professional and would wait for him to reply to my letter. They went on and on and practically bullied me to go over and ask him for an interview as he approached the bar near where we were all standing. I was either brave or naïve, but mostly, worried about losing credibility with my colleagues. As he ordered his drinks, I approached and made small talk before asking if he had received my application. He replied that he had, and we had a brief conversation about what I had achieved with my team and before I finished, he offered me the job saying that a number of people had already mentioned my name and thought I deserved the opportunity.

I stood there in shock as he walked off. Looking around for reassurance, my colleagues were looking over and giving me the thumbs up. Surreal as the interview was, my promotion to General Manager East Midlands was a fantastic experience, I was now one of only two female General Managers in the company at the time. Back in those days, there were very few women leaders in supply chain and whilst the numbers have since grown, we still need more diversity in what has always been, a very male dominated industry.

In our first year we won depot of the year. We had a great team, and it turned out to be a dream job that had never crossed my mind until someone said I couldn't do it! Remember this:

> If you're ever told you can't do something, do it anyway as you never know what might happen or how amazing it will work out. What have you got to lose?

I could go on to tell you about taking on the Area Customer Service Manager role looking after teams across six depots when the company made all the international General redundant and made us apply for Area Manager roles. Then three years later being re-instated back in the Depot General Manager positions. Or when I got to take over one of the largest international depots for a few years before becoming disillusioned, leaving TNT, and starting my own freight forwarding company. But let's face it we would be here all day, and I only have one chapter in this book!

My hope is to give you insights into why having a dream of what you want will be the catalyst to drive you forward. And whilst what I wanted back then were only materialistic things, they served me well and helped me get clear on my goals and vision for what I wanted to achieve. This is my message to you, especially if you're in the early days of your career:

> Have a vision for yourself, not necessarily a materialistic one but something that will drive you forward so you can notice the signposts and have the courage to act upon them.

It was pure serendipity how I fell into the supply chain industry and if this ever happens to you then just embrace it. I always say, 'A job is what you make it'. Embrace opportunities that present themselves, no matter how weird the situation is. You never know where it's going to lead you... Which leads me nicely on to Cornettoes.

I had taken a few months off after closing the freight forwarding company and my CV was with several agencies, all with strict instructions not to put me forward for any parcel delivery companies as I didn't want to work for anyone after working for TNT who, for me, had been the best company to work for. A change of direction to into logistics seemed appealing and I was delighted to be put forward for a position running a refrigerated warehouse for one of the big ice cream companies.

The interview was at the facility itself. I walked into the boardroom to be met by four senior managers who all seemed nice and insisted I was shown around the facility before the interview began. Their warehouse was maintained to a temperature of around -35 degrees, and it was essential to put on their safety gear which consisted of an oversized winter coat with a faux fur hood and warm looking safety boots. There I was wrapped up like an Eskimo walking through this refrigerated warehouse, thinking how amazing it was to see what went on behind the scenes of supply chain for ice-creams. I remember how exhilarated I felt from the cold and breezing back into the boardroom excitedly saying that I'll never look at a Cornetto the same again!

Leaving the interview, I felt I'd blown it after being so over-excited about Cornettoes. Imagine my surprise when the agency called that same day to say that they were really impressed and would like to offer me the position. I was relieved that I hadn't let myself down and pleased to be offered the job. However, something told me to hold fire and attend another interview I had the next day. I agreed to let the agency know my decision by the end of the week.

It's a fine line how things could have taken a different turn had I immediately accepted the position to manage a refrigerated warehouse. Listening to your gut feelings and going with your heart, even when your head is reasoning with logic to just take the job can make a profound difference on the direction your life takes. It did mine.

Despite asking the agencies not to put my CV forward to any parcel companies, one agency had the courage to ignore me (a guy named Paul who I never met) and sent my CV to what was then called Parceline. They were advertising for a National Operations Manager, and Paul thought I'd be a good fit for them. Turns out that the Director recruiting for the position thought I didn't have enough experience and rejected my CV. However, I knew none of this at the time, only finding out afterwards that my CV got passed to another Director who was looking for someone with international experience as they just launched their international air express service and need somebody to make it work operationally.

I always respect authenticity and immediately connected with the Director interviewing me who I thought would be a great mentor. And he was. I also loved that there was a female CEO at the time who inspired me immensely. In fact, every single person I met that day was friendly, open and welcoming and gave the impression that this was an amazing company to work for. I was truly delighted to get offered a position to join them.

Starting as General Manager for International within a huge domestic business, with no staff, no job description and no clue why they had 14 Gateways for 150 parcels a night, was interesting to say the least! So, I rolled up my sleeves and immediately did an assessment of each area of the business that would touch an international parcel. After completing the assessments, I left them printing off as I went to get a coffee.

The next thing I knew the Director of Hubs was summoning me to his office. I had an office on the same floor, and he had taken my reports off the print machine, saw that one of them was about his hubs and lost it with me. I stood at the end of his T-shaped desk as he bellowed at me like I was a schoolgirl who had just told him the dog ate her homework. I vividly remember thinking either I could burst into tears or sit down and talk to him. I held my composure and chose the latter, pulling a chair right up to his desk and asking him where he thought I'd gone wrong. He seemed shocked by my question and calmed down immediately. He had a reputation for being hot head. But after that day, not only was he the first person to address his department and support international, but he was also one of my best supporters and built me an office when the non-directors got asked to leave the top floor when the new CEO took over. Lesson learned:

You never know where your best allies will come from. Even in the face of adversity, showing courage can lead you to your best allies and gain you respect where you least expected.

My first member of staff was a Business Analyst, brought in at my request to take on a wide range of tasks that helped provide visibility of what we needed to tackle. Not long after, I was encouraged to take responsibility for the international finance team of four people. Then I took on another Business Analyst. Never underestimate how helpful a good BA is when you're starting something new or reviving something old!

Against all odds, my small team and I created an air service to sell. Without going into too much detail, we were tied into a very difficult contract with three suppliers, and until I could get out of this contract it was virtually impossible to create something of an express nature at a competitive price for the customer. At one point the Sales Director decided his sales team weren't going to sell air services anymore and I was asked to take responsibility of the European Road service to 'tide me over' because it apparently ran itself. Before long I could see the flaws in the service and went about turning it around by working closely with our European colleagues across the group.

Things were coming together nicely and before long I was asked to investigate why their special services department wasn't making any money and perhaps close it down. After a deep dive, I put a business plan together to suggest we keep it open and promote it to the sales teams as a retention product for customers. One of the many things I learned at TNT was to leave no stone unturned in a sales call, and always have a service to offer the customer. I believed we needed this little department and despite being told by the Sales Director it was a waste of time, my boss supported me and gave me responsibility to run it. We took it from a break-even £600k turn over to a profit making £2.2 million in just under just over 18 months.

By now my team and I were managing International Finance, European Road and Special Services. Once we were able to get out of the contract we had for air services, I was able to find a new supplier which became the turning point for a very successful beginning for our air express business. We won business from some big UK retail brands and became the go-to for the emerging e-commerce sector as we developed our services worldwide with innovative solutions and dedicated customer service.

International services were fast becoming one of the most successful departments in the company. I was now Head of International Operations and able to cultivate a real international team spirit by bringing in new people with no preconceived ideas, hungry and willing to learn. Many were fresh University Graduates and Apprentices straight from school. The average age of my team at one point was 26! Working with such a highly motivated team who were enthusiastic, creative and fun to work with was the absolute best time in my career.

At the height of our success disaster struck. I woke up one day in excruciating pain with my back, something wasn't right, but I carried on working, stupidly ignoring the pain until one day I could barely lift my left leg. I was literally dragging myself into work and being told off for coming in which was upsetting because of the effort I made to work through the pain and instead of appreciation, I was (rightly) chastised for coming in. Despite feeling hurt, this was the turning point for me to get help. Two back surgeries later and eight weeks off work I was my old self vowing never to ignore something like that again. Your health is so important. It's something money can't buy no matter how much you have. Well-being is the buzz word these days but it's just a word unless you're prepared to put the effort in and do something about your physical health. Trust me, one day you won't have a choice. I became a devout Pilates student tight to this day.

By now the combined international services was quarter of a billion £ business and the most profitable part of DPD UK at that time. Yet, despite being bigger and more profitable than other departments, there was still no international voice on the Board. It seems I had hit a glass ceiling. I made an appointment with the HR Director to gain advice on what skills were needed to get promoted to the board. We had a positive conversation but there was very little he could do as it was the decision of the CEO. He then asked if there were any training courses that appealed to me. I remember thinking, that if I put in the effort in to work on myself, I would come out the other side and either this company would promote me to a director, or some other company would.

I decided to pursue studies in NLP (Neurolinguistic Programming). This brought my fascination of the power of the mind together nicely. My curiosity had never left since that day in Somerset where I found the book by Dr. Joseph Murphy and many books later, a whole new world opened up for me. NLP helped me realise that there is so much more we are capable of and so much more we can achieve once we learn how to re-model our thought patterns and adopt strategies for success.

The course I attended also gave me the opportunity to study for a qualification in coaching with the ILM (Institute of Leadership Management) I just needed a few volunteers to help me get the required number of hours of documented coaching. Several members of my team were more than happy to volunteer and even after qualifying that year, they still wanted to continue what we had started. That's when I had the idea to launch a coaching and mentoring programme across the department, something that continued for many years and a program that elevated team members into being mentors themselves. I'm proud to say that many of those that took part went on to become Managers, General Managers and Heads of Department, paying much credit to the program I had set up.

NLP gave me the knowledge, inspiration and a shift in perspective of who I was and how I showed up as a leader. Whilst I hadn't given up on my ambition to be promoted to the board of directors to represent international, I had let it go to the back of my mind whilst I continued to study NLP to Master Practitioner and Master Coach level.

It was a hot July day, and sitting in my office, with no air conditioning I was waiting for a visit from the CEO, who was coming over to have a chat about my department. I didn't think anything of it and was hoping to leave on time to get to a Pilates class, but he still hadn't arrived. I called his PA and was told he was on his way and before long we were sat around a small table in my office talking about the team and other things. Slumped in my chair getting hotter and more impatient as the conversation continued, I suddenly felt the questions he was asking were the type you asked in an interview. Instinct kicked in I quickly sat upright and answered his questions honestly and authentically to which he replied, "and that's why I want you on my board of directors!"

Dumbfounded, I asked him to repeat what he had said as I couldn't believe it. After taking so long to get to this point in my career, it felt unreal. I couldn't wait to tell my husband; it was humbling and emotional when Keith told me how proud he was of me. No-one had ever told me that before and I will always remember how valued it made me feel. Now, whenever the opportunity arises, I don't hesitate to pay the compliment forward when somebody deserves the recognition.

Being on the board of a £2 billion company as the Director of International Operations wasn't always easy. We had to fight to get on people's agenda as domestic was always the priority, but it was still a fantastic opportunity which I whole heartedly embraced and for several years we continued to thrive as a team as we enjoyed double digit growth, along with lots of recognition and success. Then Brexit hit.

It was the worst experience of my career and a difficult time for everybody in the country never mind our company. My team and I, plus a dedicated project team were tasked with building an import/export operation from scratch with our own Customs clearance to manage the 100 plus trailers a day crossing the channel. To say it was hard is an understatement and too long-winded to include here, but what I will say is something really good came out of it.

Shortly after launching our new Brexit operation, my boss received a call from Boris Winkelmann, the CEO and Chairman of the Geopost group, owned by the esteemed La Poste Group in Paris. He was determined to expand internationally across the group and recognised my courage and reputation as ideal for the task. Like many others, I admired him greatly for his remarkable character and dynamic enthusiasm—a true powerhouse in making things happen. So, I eagerly accepted the opportunity to join his team as the International Managing Director.

Leaving my beloved international team in the UK was a difficult decision, but after taking the International Division from practically nothing to over £310 million revenue, I was ready for a new challenge and the timing felt right.

Six months into the new job, devastating news sent shockwaves throughout the group: Boris had tragically passed away. He was in his early fifties and whilst we all felt the impact of him going too soon, you can only imagine the profound loss his wife and family were experiencing. This tragedy made us all reflect on how precious time is with our loved ones and the importance of appreciating every day.

The next couple of years flew by as my team and I established a European import/export operation in six countries, designed and implemented insightful reports and built an enthusiastic global community of International Ambassadors. Despite our progress, the premature loss of our leader was always in the back of my mind and served as a poignant reminder to consider what I truly wanted out of life.

In late 2022, I received a newsletter promoting a course called 'Multiple Brain Integration Techniques' (*m*BIT). A course designed by the visionary creators of *m*Braining; Grant Soosalu and Marvin Oka, who had collaborated and combined their expertise to develop a unique coaching method that blends modern neuroscience, neuro-linguistic programming (NLP), and ancient wisdom that acknowledges the existence of multiple neural networks within the human body.

I was intrigued and felt a strong pull to sign up.

The course was incredibly enlightening and emphasised the benefits of alignment between the head, heart, and gut. I learned what it means when you hear phrases like "listen to your heart" or "trust your gut," and discovered the profound significance of our three core operating systems, how they communicate and how their alignment can transform our decision-making and overall well-being. As a corporate thinker (head) and doer (gut) I had never taken the time to tune in and listen to my heart. By day four on the course something had shifted in me that was hard to explain.

Three months later, sat in one of our global meetings, I felt like somebody had lifted a veil and for the first time saw why this environment was no longer fulfilling for me. The layers of corporate masks built up over the years no longer fit and I realised that my heart just wasn't in it anymore. I craved authenticity and heart-centred leadership, not competitive egotism. When I arrived home from the trip, I told my husband I was going to resign. He smiled and said, "about time!" For the first time in my life, I listened to my heart and decided to retire from corporate life to pursue other interests. Although everyone was surprised by my decision to leave a successful career, it didn't deter me as my mind (or minds!) were made up. They gave me a great send-off and some wonderful gifts and memorable messages that will always be treasured. The feedback I received helped me realise how much of a difference I'd made in some people's lives and could continue to do so in this next chapter.

At the start of my career, I didn't always know what I wanted to do, but I always knew what sort of person I wanted to be; authentic, honest and helpful to others. The desire for success originally stemmed from a need to survive, earn money and buy things to make me look and feel successful. But as time passed, I gained a deeper sense of self and a desire for purpose and a drive to make a difference.

My next step was to spend time learning how to teach *m*Braining, so travelled to the South of France and became one of only 200 trainers worldwide certified to train and certify others in this powerful coaching modality that helps people become better leaders, coaches and mentors. With my corporate experience in senior leadership roles and the extensive training I had invested in over the years, I knew I was well equipped to make a bigger impact, and this was the path I was meant to follow.

Throughout the years, I've encountered my share of negative people who tried to pull me down and hold me back, but I had courage to keep pushing forward, even when times were tough. The resilience I developed as a child has been invaluable in my career, especially in the field of supply chain where quick thinking and adaptability is essential. My upbringing fostered a sense of independence and belief that I could achieve anything I put my mind to. That's why this next chapter of my life is so important. Sometimes I feel that time is running out and I may not accomplish everything I hope to, but I still have an abundance of energy, enthusiasm and passion to make my later living years have purpose and meaning. This is my why.

My company: MDS Alignment Ltd was born out of a deep passion and calling to make a difference. I genuinely love what I do and the people I have the privilege to help. Every day, I feel immensely grateful to share my life with the most wonderful human being on the planet…my husband Keith. His unwavering support and love helped shape who I am today. He has stood by my side, supported everything I wanted to do and been there during the toughest times when I felt I couldn't go on. Be grateful for those around you cheering you on; they may be few, but they are there.

If you're feeling lost or uncertain about your direction in life, I hope my story inspires you. I stumbled into supply chain, embraced every opportunity, worked hard, and took risks, and I want you to find the hope and courage to do the same. And remember…a job is what you make it. You never have to be defined by a job description, a boss or a company. It's about how you show up, what you want to create, and the value you bring to the table. Make it a win/win situation, where both you and the company benefit from what you contribute. And most importantly:

> Have the courage to embrace the opportunities that come your way and pursue the things that make your heart sing. It's in those moments that you'll find true fulfilment and purpose.

I'm happier now than I've ever been; running a successful business that truly reflects my passions – Executive Coaching, Leadership Training and Business Consultancy. In addition to that, I've found immense joy in working with schools as a certified mentor, helping students navigate their journeys. There's something very special about connecting with the younger generation, they have so much to teach us and mentoring them has become one of the most meaningful ways I give back.

I'm deeply grateful for the courage it took to leave the corporate world and start my own business at a time when many choose to slow down. But here's the truth…I'm far from slowing down. I'm just getting started, and my heart is all in.

The best is yet to come!

The Logistics Legends

Mandy Deakin-Snell
Founder and CEO of MDS Alignment Ltd.

Supply Chain Expert, Fractional Chief Strategy Officer, Business Consultant, Executive Coach

Mandy Deakin-Snell is a distinguished executive with an impressive background in senior leadership roles at globally acclaimed corporations within the supply chain sector. With a proven track record in people development, Mandy has consistently demonstrated her ability to cultivate thriving, award-winning teams.

As the Director of International Operations at **DPD UK**, Mandy **won multiple awards,** establishing herself as a **high-performing specialist** in international export/import operations and bespoke customer solutions within the global e-commerce sector. Her exemplary leadership led to her promotion to International **Managing Director** of Geopost Group in Paris, a division of the renowned La Poste company. Here, she spear-headed the international division, assembled a high-calibre global team, and spearheaded the implementation of innovative technology to successfully launch new European import/

export gateways, bespoke financial reporting systems, and comprehensive sales training programs, fostering an international community of leaders.

In 2023, **Mandy** transitioned from her illustrious corporate career to pursue her passion for empowering leaders to achieve **holistic success** in both their business and personal lives. She founded **MDS Alignment Ltd.**, a catalyst for global enterprises seeking optimised solutions in supply chain management and people development. As a trusted advisor and consultant, Mandy provides strategic guidance and insights to enhance business efficiencies and promote authentic leadership. She offers senior-level counsel to emerging ventures, leveraging her expertise in startup dynamics and cultivating a company culture rooted in **authenticity** and **heart-centred compassion**.

Mandy specialises in developing cohesive and high-performing teams within corporate environments. Utilising her extensive experience to guide busy executives through transformative change, both professionally and personally. As a Certified mBIT Coach and Coach Trainer in **Multiple Brain Integration Techniques** (a blend of neuroscience-based research and practical coaching methods), and a Master Coach in **NLP (Neuro-Linguistic Programming)**, Mandy offers a unique approach to making wiser, more sustainable decisions.

Mandy Deakin-Snell's visionary leadership and expertise make her a sought-after authority in the fields of supply chain management, people development, and executive coaching. Her commitment to excellence and innovative thinking continue to drive impactful results for global enterprises.

Reach out to Mandy: linkedin.com/in/mandydeakin

Chapter 4

Ashwin Didwania

My story

I had a dream as a child...

I Would Always Paint My Dream... ...
We'll come to that part a bit later—but for now, let's start with my childhood.

I just wanted to make it through the day without being scolded.

Growing up in 1970s–80s India, academics were the only measure by which a child was judged. You were a "good" or "bad" boy purely based on your grades, not your behaviour. In this environment, a weak student like me struggled with immense pressure and acceptance issues related to my difficult time in school.

Since my grades were weak, "playtime" was out of the question. However, I was fortunate that my parents, especially my father, encouraged me to engage in sports—probably the only thing I was half good at—and in this, I found a lot of joy.

My teenage years were more of the same, with the stress of grades and difficult study cycles, but sports provided comfort as a hobby, and I lived in a strict but loving home. One of my favourite subjects in school was art. Not because I was good at it, but because I could "paint" my own canvas.

Every time I had to draw a "home," I always drew one with a water body or stream nearby, meadows, and... wait for it... an airplane parked in the garden. (That was the dream I alluded to earlier.)

Don't ask me why or how I had this constant dream—I can't explain it myself. How could a boy from a crowded Indian city, living in a relatively tiny flat, draw such a picture of "home" (see the attached picture)? Little did I know, I was sowing the seeds of something for my future...

I just didn't know it yet.

Introduction to Business & Panalpina

Barely making it through formal education with a graduate degree in commerce, it was time for me to follow in my family's footsteps into the logistics industry.

I started by working with Hanjin Shipping in Bombay in 1993, and it was a period of deep learning—going to the port, moving containers, planning vessels, and interacting with people from all strata of society. What I learned during this period was humility and appreciation for the hard work and long hours put in by the port workers and ship handlers.

At that time, our company, New Globe, was the exclusive handling agent for Panalpina (a Swiss MNC, now acquired by DSV) in India.

In 1994, I began working with Panalpina in their Singapore office, learning the ropes across operations, accounting, and sales (sales was, is, and will always remain my favourite part of logistics). This period exposed me to the global scale and approach in freight forwarding, giving me a bird's-eye view of the industry.

Returning to India in 1996 after my stint at Panalpina, I joined the family business. My first task was to "collect" an overdue invoice from one of our clients.

Now, for the uninitiated, no business school or book will ever teach you what I believe is the hardest lesson in business: collecting your money. This story is worth sharing as it left a deep impression, guiding me toward future success.

Given the "outstanding statement," I went to my client's office to discuss the matter. What followed is comical when I retell it now, but at the time, it was a painful lesson.

As I shared the statement, the client said nothing—then simply found every excuse not to pay, delay, find fault, and exasperate me.

Things took a turn for the worse when I tried to "reason with" the client toward a settlement. The client simply blew up (as if expecting it—and I played right into his hands). The whole situation was a "set up" by the client to push all the buttons, leading to an argument. And in India, this usually means the client is upset and will not pay, feeling "insulted" that someone had the audacity to ask for something as petty as a "payment."

I went into the client's office expecting a pleasant interaction and settlement of a due invoice but came out with empty pockets and insults instead. I know this is an extreme case, but it was my first, and it shaped my learnings deeply.

In that moment, I learned that being in business meant a delicate balancing act of dealing with various sensitive people—clients, employees, customs, government staff, etc.—all requiring skill in reading a situation, honing your intuition, leaving your ego at the door, and building consensus and communication with all. Sometimes, that even meant making a donkey a king for the day.

This lesson has served me well in building my business and relationships. I thank that difficult client for giving me a valuable lesson in business management. Pity that a few years later, the client's business went bankrupt. That was his karma.

Business Setbacks, Learnings, and Getting Back Up

It had barely been two years since I joined the business and was trying to learn the ropes when I was struck by two life-defining events in the same year: 1999.

The first, and the most joyous for me, was the birth of my first-born son, Aman.

The second was devastating news that Panalpina, our partner and contributor to 90% of our revenue, would start their own operations in India. (Hint: We were on the verge of losing 90% of our revenue, and I was about to become a father.)

This came to pass, and I was all of 25, with a young child to be responsible for. Overnight, I went from being part of a profitable, stable company to one in deep red, facing a long climb back out of the hole.

The next few years were a period of tremendous learning and experience. It was like starting from scratch—putting my head down, taking one step at a time, and just keeping on moving.

It also inadvertently taught me resilience and built a very thick skin, able to withstand general stress and difficult situations. This period also marked the beginning of my spiritual journey through prayer and following the Art of Living organization (a spiritual organization based in India).

Getting Back on Top & to the Moment Right Now

Through the 2000s, it was a slow but steady build-up of our business, and I wish to highlight a turning point. In 2012, an opportunity came to kick off the air consolidation arm of NGL. Although I did not have the experience, I simply had the will and an idea. Thus, NCS (Neutral Consolidation Services—sister firm of New Globe Logistik) was born. Within the first three months, revenues started coming in, and we have not looked back since. After years of struggle, finally, New Globe and its sister concern, NCS, both suddenly turned around.

What the experience taught me was to follow your gut and intuition as a businessman.

How do you develop intuition? By going inwards through the process of meditation.

At the age of 45, in 2019, a life event caused me to shift my base country to the Netherlands.

What seemed very scary at first—new country, language, and work environment, away from my familiar place of work and home—turned out to be an opportunity to develop myself by overcoming those challenges and thriving.

I learned a new language, Dutch, and used the COVID period to fulfil my lifelong dream of learning to fly and become a pilot. It forced me to digitize and professionalize my work by getting in and promoting a fabulous management team. Along the journey, I learned many lessons that apply to work and life.

The lessons I learned in flying also apply to business, and I like to share three main takeaways:

Conquer Your Fears:

Let me share a secret—I have always been afraid of flying. It was a love-hate relationship; I love planes and the romance of it, but turbulence made me a nervous wreck. How could I possibly be calm when a storm hits? As a pilot, this was the difference between life and death. However, my love of flying won over my fears. I had to work through my fears during my training to finally earn my pilot's license.

In business, too, there are many scenarios that are scary, leaving us nervous and afraid. But this is an opportunity for us to conquer our own demons and overcome them. As the famous author Adam Grant said, "Personality is how you show up on a good day; character is how you tackle a bad one." Overcoming my fears and breaking my comfort zone led to character building that applies to both flying and business.

One Step at A Time, always:

When I first understood the amount of work (flying hours, exams, study, preparations) required to qualify as a pilot, it threw me off balance. In my head, I created 100 reasons (all valid) why this was not possible, ranging from the usual "I don't have the time" to "It's too much work," etc.

At this point, my dear wife gave me one piece of advice: "Take one day at a time and start. Be consistent and disciplined, and the rest will follow—focus on a small daily step." So, after clarifying my goal, I simply put my head down and took one step a day toward it. By the time I looked up again—two and a half years later—I was a pilot.

In the same way, when building a business, the large goals can seem very far away and unachievable. Instead of focusing on the goals, focus on the next step to achieve them. Take it one day at a time, be consistent and disciplined, and I promise—you will achieve your goal.

Have Faith, Do the Right Karma, and Allow the Results to Manifest When They Will:

"You have the right to the action, not to the fruits of the action." This is a line from the Bhagavad Gita (a holy book for Hindus). Simply put, we only have control over our own actions and activities; we don't have control over the results. Usually, we are impatient for the results and make rash decisions we regret later. I am a firm believer in the law of karma—that one has to do the right action and perform one's duty in the best manner possible. Sometimes you are rewarded immediately; sometimes not.

The importance is to trust the process and understand that the universe works in strange ways. In the end, honest work is always rewarded. Much like planting a seed and watering it daily—it may take years to show any sign of life, but by being consistent, one fine day, a tree will be there bearing many fruits. Be patient and work hard.

I applied this to my flying journey and continue to apply it daily to my business journey.

Now and future

Today, I Am Proud of the Way the Group Is Shaping Up

We now have four entities: NGL India, NGL Sri Lanka, NCS India (the consolidation arm), and Motus BV (an e-commerce and distribution firm in the EU), each delivering solutions and using IT to add value for our clients. We provide visibility, CO_2 monitoring, control, predictability, and MIS across their supply chains, making us a valuable partner in logistics.

Along the journey, I have made friends and done business all over the world, overcome business and personal challenges, and been blessed to work alongside an amazing team led handsomely by my CEO and partner, Ms. Nomita Kothari.

The horizon holds deeper employee participation in the business through profit sharing, expansion of our footprint to Eastern Europe, ensuring green compliance, and, most importantly, building a culture that adds value to clients, employees, and society. This is achieved by delivering on our values of Trust, Transparency, Teamwork, and Responsibility, and by living up to our legacy of delivering promises since 1950.

Looking ahead, we aim for a significant pivot towards AI and technology, focusing on serving our clients better with transparency, speed, accuracy, and dependability. We have already developed our own systems that allow clients and agents to book, monitor, track, and generate reports in a customized manner, making working with us a smooth and enjoyable experience.

I believe there are certain tasks that can never be replaced by technology, such as quality customer service, sales, and thinking outside the box. Our goal as a firm is to stand on the dual pillars of technology and human service, delivering the best of both worlds.

For me personally, the horizon includes developing spiritually and combining spirituality with business, engaging in society, and ensuring growth for all stakeholders and clients within the NGL orbit.

The journey of excellence is the reward in itself, not the arrival at a destination.

My learning is that we don't need the right conditions, mood, or situation to succeed; we simply need to show up and keep doing. In the process, we overcome what we thought we could not, and therein lies the magic of growth—not in "perfection" but in the process of "imperfection."

Quoting something I once read: "It's the struggle of the climb that makes the view from the top of the mountain breathtaking."

Team photo – NGL.

Plane in my garden (my dream come true)

Pilot photo

Ashwin Didwania
Founder and CEO of New Globe Group

Ashwin Didwania is a seasoned executive with over 30 years of experience in the global logistics industry. His career began in 1993 with Hanjin Shipping in India, where he quickly developed a strong foundation in maritime logistics. From 1994 to 1996, Ashwin expanded his expertise internationally by working with Panalpina in Singapore, further honing his skills in freight forwarding and global trade operations.

Since joining **New Globe Group** in 1996, Ashwin has been a pivotal force in the company's growth, leading key initiatives that strengthened partnerships, alliances, and both the export and import sectors of the business. Under his leadership, New Globe achieved **ISO certification in 2003**, marking a significant milestone in its commitment to quality and operational excellence.

Ashwin's forward-thinking approach has led him to spearhead the expansion of the New Globe Group through the establishment of sister firms such as **NCS India**, a neutral consolidation company; **NGL**

Lanka, a freight forwarding firm in Sri Lanka; and **Motus BV**, an e-commerce, warehousing, and distribution centre in the Netherlands. In recent years, he has focused on the digitization of the NGL Group, ensuring that the company remains at the forefront of innovation by offering **more accurate, user-friendly, and eco-friendly** services.

A graduate of **Sydenham College** in Mumbai with a Bachelor's degree in Commerce, Ashwin balances his professional endeavours with his passions outside of work. He is an avid sportsman, marathon runner, and licensed pilot who enjoys flying in his spare time. Fluent in **English, Hindi, and Dutch**, Ashwin brings a multicultural perspective, having been born into a family with Thai and Indian heritage, and now shares his life with his Dutch wife and their three sons.

Beyond the corporate world, Ashwin is an active member of the **Rotary Club**, where he is involved in various charitable projects. He is also a dedicated practitioner of spiritual development, closely following the teachings of the **Art of Living Foundation** to integrate mindfulness and well-being into both his personal life and corporate leadership style.

Ashwin Didwania's vision, multicultural background, and focus on sustainable growth and digitization continue to shape the future of global logistics through his leadership at New Globe Group.

Reach out to Ashwin: linkedin.com/in/ashwindidwania

Chapter 5

Gilbert Ernest

My story

No matter how you look at it, life is just a series of decisions that you make. You can call it fate, but the things you chose to do will always shape your future. Things may happen to you, which are outside your control, and which at the time may seem catastrophic, but it's how you decide to react to them that will determine where you end up. And those little or big decisions bring along a constant change, which you need to embrace to be able to grow positively. My life has been full of those moments that would eventually lead me to write this book.

My name is Gilbert Ernest, and I am the owner and managing director of GE International Forwarding Pty Ltd. A small freight forwarding company based in Melbourne Australia. Owning my own business, despite all the challenges that come with it, has brought me such fulfillment. I am in control of my own destiny, and I can say that my life is beautiful, stressful sometimes, but worth it. I can afford things I never could in my previous life, and I travel the world every year discovering new countries, making new friends and connections. More importantly, I am contributing to the growth of my clients' businesses by helping them streamlining their business expenses. I have a lot of satisfied customers who are so happy that they recommend my company to their friends and connections. But my life has not always been like that. It took me some real bad times to turn me into the person I am today.

In the days before owning my business. I was just your typical employee, following orders, always doing the right thing for the company, though never really seeing the rewards. I had a few promotions into managerial positions along the way, sure, but my destiny was in the hands of someone else. Nevertheless, I believed in the system, and I was pretty "secure" in that comfort zone, and I took it all for granted, until the bubble burst. And it did with a real big bang.

… and this is how the story enfolds…

It all started on a small island called Rodriques, situated about 350 miles to the east of the Island Republic of Mauritius, in the Indian Ocean, where I was born at 7:00 AM on a Friday morning, 14 February 1958. Rodrigues was and still is a dependency of Mauritius.

My father was a police officer and was on duty in Rodrigues from Mauritius at the time. My mother was your traditional stay-at-home wife, looking after the children. As the duty was going to last a few years, the whole family came with my father to Rodrigues. My parents, who already had three daughters, were so happy when I was born, for at last they had a son. They will go on to have another three daughters after me, which would leave me being the only boy in the family for 8 years.

When I turned 2, my father was recalled to Mauritius where I would spend my childhood and young adulthood.

That time of my life was very simple. We were not rich, but we had everything we needed though without any great luxury. We lived in a little town by the sea name Mahebourg, and I would spend a lot of time as a young boy, at the at the beach, or going fishing with the local fishermen in the lagoon. Just imagine the blue sky, warm sun above, slight sea breeze, coconut trees – Paradise in fact. Life was sweet. Or was it? A lot of the time I would get into trouble with my dad for not being back at home in time and not doing my homework. And I would cop a real butt whooping. The good old days. But being the only boy in the family had its advantages, as no need to say, I was spoilt rotten. I was king of the castle and almost anything I wanted was given to me. Even when my brother was born, I would remain the favourite of the family. As a teenager, I never had to do anything at home. My sisters did everything for me. Unfortunately, this sweet life would come to a sad end. My parents ended up divorcing when I was 16 years of age which brought a lot of misery to my siblings' and my life. We were caught in the crossfire of a rapidly declining relationship. But we comforted and looked after each other the best we could.

From an early age I was drawn to music and my grandmother taught me how to play the harmonica. I had the dream of one day playing in a band, but My mum did not want to have a bar of it (no pun intended) as she always wanted me to be a doctor or lawyer or something like that. But all I wanted was a guitar, which she refused to buy me until I turned 18. While waiting for that day, at school I hung around with some musicians who would lend me a guitar over the weekends. I began self-teaching myself guitar with some valuable tips from one of my neighbors who was already an experienced player. She really helped me train my musical ear. We used to jam a lot and before long, I could play the guitar very well. In the end, my mum also had her desire partially, as I graduated high school with a diploma in Accounts and bookkeeping. I was supposed to become an accountant, but it never happened.

I realized I could sing when the school put on a talent show which

I joined first as only a guitar player. But it turned out the show lacked some male singer, and my teacher asked me to sing. I hesitated at first because I had never sung in public before. I used to accompany myself while playing guitar at home, but that was only to learn the songs on guitar. All my friends told me I could do it. I eventually bowed to peer pressure and sang Neil Diamond's "Song sung blue". Unfortunately, there was no standing ovation, as I was so nervous with stage fright. But the performance was ok. After the show I got together with a couple of fellow students and started a band, playing mostly rock and roll. We did not have many gigs at all, and we were taken advantage of by an agent who made us play for a meal and took all the money for himself. But my journey as a performing musician had started. It wasn't until 1975 that I truly got a break as singer / performer. The band got a contract with an agent who got us gigs every week, playing at tourists resorts like the Club Med and Le Meridien, and sometimes playing at weddings etc. I would later join another band which became very popular on the island, named The Revivals. But I will leave this story for another time.

In 1977 I turned nineteen and got a job at a shipping Company, in Port Louis Mauritius, Rogers and Co., Ltd., and my career in the industry began as a disbursement clerk, in the ships agency of the company. We were the agents of shipping lines like P & O, MSC, OOCL, The Shipping Corporation of India and the South African Line, Unicorn Lines. My job was various. One duty was boarding the vessels at time of arrival and facilitate the Customs and Quarantine inspections. But most of the time, because of my diploma in Accounts, my duties were to compile and prepare disbursement accounts for money we had spent while the vessel was in Port on behalf of the owners and charterers. Other duties were, to put it in the words of my letter of appointment, anything that may be required of me by the company. One of those was to help with the repatriation of sailors who had completed their contracts or who were sent home because of illness or some other reason. All this interaction with people of different nationalities made me become a people's person. I became very comfortable with talking to people from different cultures.

These were the days before computers, email and mobile phones. I remember we had to type the ship's manifest on a typewriter and hand it to the captain just before sailing. And every Friday we had to work overtime in the Telex Room, sending various messages to our principals around the world. I got to also learn CB radio and communicated with vessels at anchor before they berthed.

This was also the time before shipping containers and all the cargo would be shipped as breakbulk. Ships would stay in port more than a week to discharge imports and load exports. The first container would not arrive until 1979 and the first vessel to carry them for our company, was a Mediterranean Shipping Company vessel, Alexa II. I remember the stevedores going on strike as there would be no more long overtime as there was in the breakbulk days. That year we also had our first FAK from India and it was a nightmare. None of the mark and numbers, carton count or anything at all matched. We had to open the cartons to see what was in them before we could deliver to the right consignee. Customs had a nightmare with this container.

The company also regularly put on Cabaret shows for the staff at which I would perform. And at one of those shows, it was the first and only time my mother would see me perform live. Other times, she would see me on TV only. My father, bless his soul, has sadly never seen me perform.

In 1982, I got married to my first wife Josiane, and out of this marriage, two beautiful girls were born, Carine and Valerie. The ensuing five years would be very happy, although not so easy. There was no more mum and sisters to look after me and I had to learn how to cook and iron and all the other chores that come with the household of a young family. We also had to put up with sleepless nights, dirty nappies, sick babies etc.... those of you with children, you know how it goes.

In 1987 I made my first life changing decision. And that was to migrate to Sydney Australia with my wife and two very young daughters. And this, despite my career at Rogers & Co Ltd was on the up. I was soon to be made manager of a department, and my singing career was skyrocketing with the Revivals. We performed every week at high class venues and at the weddings of the rich and famous on the island. We also had TV appearances. I was leaving certainty and comfort zone for the unknown. I was leaving behind my mother and my family, for the promise of a better life for my children. What if it does not work out? what if we did not adapt to Australian life? I had all these questions in my mind. But never once did I let doubt creep in. I had to take that leap of faith. And on the 17 September 1987, I found myself on a Singapore Airline Flight with my wife and two daughters bound for Sydney Australia. The adventure had begun.

In the beginning we stayed with one of my wife's aunts, who was our sponsor for our visa. But I was to learn the hard way that guests were like fish and that they really stink after 3 days and circumstances had it that soon we would be forced to find our own place to live. Which was fine, I do like my independence, and we spent our first Christmas in Australia in December 1987, in a 2-bedroom flat in the suburb of Auburn, west of Sydney.

Although I was lucky to immediately get a job at a shipping company as an Export documentation Clerk, it was not easy coping with a completely different culture and being away from the immediate family. But we made the best of the situation, my wife made some friends at the local mother's club, and I joined a jazz trio.

We then made the big mistake of buying a house too early, while not yet properly established in Australia, and that put a lot of pressure on us. My wife at that time was not working and the money I was earning at my job was not enough to cover the mortgage repayments and our household expenses. So, I had to work overtime almost every day and played in the band on the weekends to make money. Luckily, the band had a residency at a Wedding Reception Place called Cheddington, north of Sydney, where we sometimes played 5 gigs in one weekend during the wedding season. We went on with our lives, making some more friends and slowly became used to the change of lifestyle and culture. We became Australian Citizens in November 1990 and never looked back. At work everything was going fine. I would be promoted regularly, going from Exports to Customer service department to Systems supervisor. Which is funny as before coming to Australia, I had never seen a computer in my life. So, when I started working on computers, I was curious and excited to learn about systems, which was noticed by my boss and who supported me to get some courses.

In 1992, I made my second life changing decision. The company I was working for had the position of Freight Manager open in the head office in Melbourne, Victoria. I applied for the job and got it. That would be the start of events that would change my life completely. We sold our house and moved the whole family to Melbourne. Unfortunately, as we did not have enough equity in the house, we had to sell at a loss which put us deeply into dept. We once again had to put up with changes. In culture, environment, weather, Australian Rules Football, and everything else Victoria had different from New South Wales. I was also going to quickly learn that being a non-Victorian, it would be very difficult for me to be accepted by the staff and other colleagues, especially as I got this managerial job above other Victorians who applied for it too. And to be honest, I failed royally at the job. The staff had no respect for me, no matter what I did. I was someone from Sydney trying to tell people in Melbourne what to do. What was I expecting? It does not work that way. After less than a year, I was demoted and went back to being a booking clerk. I was so disillusioned and began to hate my job. I became depressed and I neglected my duty as a husband and father while I wallowed in self-pity. I was going through a really bad time, and I had no one to talk to. My wife, instead of being supportive and understanding what I was going through, began nagging me and we started fighting all the time. Eventually it became all too much, and all that pressure brought our relationship to an end. We separated in 1993 and would divorce 1 year later. I was so devastated, as I felt like such a failure. I became even more depressed and hated my life even more. So, I tried to look for solace elsewhere and concentrated on music. I needed someone to give me that little nudge and tell me everything would be alright. I needed something to take that darkness in my life away. I began playing in pubs and hotels where one day I met the woman who would become my second wife.

And suddenly, life started to get a bit better. I got made redundant from my work and, with a friend's help, got a job as a Sales Representative with another Shipping Agency called Union Bulkships that same week. Union Bulkships would shortly be bought by a small Shipping Line called ANZDL. With ANZDL I would truly find my calling. I was a born salesman, and I did not know it. I was immediately successful in signing up several new clients. I was breaking down doors like no tomorrow and I quickly made a name for myself in the industry.

It was not long before I was offered a sales Management position, my career there would be very successful. I won the award for Sales executive of the year, 3 years in a row, and was happy with myself. I also started getting involved in charities and organized the very first "Shipping Ball" in Victoria, giving all the proceeds of the ball to the Royal Children Hospital. This ball became very popular, and I began organizing one every year. Until it all came to an end as you will soon see. ANZDL was bought by another Big Shipping Company where politics was rife. It was who you sucked up to that would make you advance. And there were a lot of suckers around. I refused to be one of those. I know my strength and did not need to be the boss's pet.

Amidst all this turmoil, I met my second wife, Nicole, and we would marry in 1996. From that marriage were born two handsome boys. Sebastien and Daniel. We bought a big house in Rowville, Southeast of Melbourne, and my wife started a wedding planner business. I also started a band playing mostly in the wedding industry and would go on to win various awards as best live entertainment. My wife did a good job at managing the band and getting our name out there. Everything was fantastic. As this life went on, I began feeling even more comfortable and taking things for granted. I would never have imagined how all this would come crumbling down in a big way. The wind of change would be blowing soon and sweep me away in a downward spiral.

As I was successful at my job and with the band, a couple of times, my wife suggested that I start my own business, but I was too smug in my comfort zone and brushed off the idea by finding all sorts of excuses. There was no need to start a business, I had a very good job, company car, a house and a beautiful family, what more could I want?

In 2003 things in my life started going downhill again. ANZDL had been sold by then, and I found myself having to play dodge ball with politics in the new company. Work colleagues started stabbing each other in the back, vying for a small promotion that became available. The atmosphere began to deteriorate, and the work environment was not enjoyable anymore. Gone were the days of ANZDL. My personal life was no better, my marriage began falling apart for reasons I never understood then, and still don't understand today, as in my mind, I was always doing the right thing in my marriage as in my job. But one day my wife said she did not want to be with me anymore and that I should leave. Despite all the counseling and therapy sessions, this marriage also ended in divorce in 2003. And I lost everything once again in the process. Money, property, my kids. Everything. Being the nice guy, or stupid, that I am, I gave my wife the house, the car, the kids and even paid the lawyers.

The effect of the divorce was going to be even worse in the coming 2 years. I began losing my motivation at work, trying hard not to show it in my output. I was also short on money, as I spent most of it on divorce settlement and on child support payments. One again there was a darkness in my life which was so mentally draining that I found myself making quite a few stupid decisions. One of those was driving under the influence of alcohol in August 2005 and losing my license for 15 months. This was going to be a blessing in disguise, though at the time it was a disaster. I was a wreck and was really in a dark place.

After losing my license, the company was at first accommodating and said I could keep my job, whether I took taxis or public transport to visit clients. Which I did. But all the wins had dried up. I was not signing up for any new business anymore, I had lost my mojo, and found it more and more difficult to breath at work, with politics and all. Even singing in the band began to bore me. I was down and soon to be out. Then came the "coup de grace" as we say in French. It happened that another Major Shipping line bought the one I was working for, and they were offering voluntary redundancy to the sales force as they were merging the two companies. There was my opportunity to get out of this place and refocus on my life with a redundancy package. I had been working for the last year and the money was going to be in the 100's of thousand. So, I jumped on the opportunity and put my hand up to receive the package. But what I got was a big kick on the head. The "powers that be" in the company, not wanting to pay me out for 12 years of loyal service, suddenly decided that not having a license did not allow me to fulfill my job and instead of giving me the package, they fired me instantly. Without even paying me one cent, on 18 November 2005. 1 month before Christmas. That morning, I had a meeting with one of my big clients and to my surprise, the branch manager wanted to be invited to the meeting. At first, I did not understand why, but I went along with it. When we got back to the office, he called me into his office and gave me the news. I hit a brick wall at 100 KPH. I still remember him asking me if I would be alright. Yeah right, what a stupid question. I answered "yes, what about you?" and was soon escorted off the premises. I went home and cried my eyes out with anger and feelings of having been used.

Suddenly I had no money and nowhere to stay, as I could not pay my rent. My rent was paid until the end of December, but I had no money to pay for January. My whole world was falling apart. But strangely somehow, I did not feel defeated, something inside was telling me it was going to be alright. I could not see a way out but deep inside I knew that I had to hang on and not give up. Help would come from somewhere unexpected. God works in mysterious ways and my first wife took pity on me and offered me a place to stay until I could get back on my feet. What do you know? Forever grateful. Thank you, thank you, thank you Josiane!

I spent a few months looking for jobs, where they would tell me that I was too old or too experienced etc., etc.... I enrolled with an employment agency and ended up working some casual jobs at a couple of freight forwarding companies, as a clerk. As I had no license, I had to go to these jobs on my bicycle. This was so humiliating for me at the start. Here was I, an experienced shipping professional and successful State Sales Manager for a Major Shipping Line working as a fill-in clerk. But I decided to see the positive sides of things and began to learn about the Forwarding Industry. Having worked all my life for shipping lines, I really did not know much about forwarding, customs and related services. This led me to landing a permanent job at a small Freight Forwarding company in 2009, which I will not name for privacy reasons. Although I was very successful in this job as well, it was not going to be a pleasant time for me. The owner of the company was a very obnoxious person. I thought he was a nice man until he started showing his bad side. He was micromanaging me and was breaching my privacy by having my emails redirected to him, he was always fighting with shipping lines, agents, clients, over insignificant amounts of money. In the 3 years that I worked for him; he changed about five agents in the USA and had this war of words with our New Zealand agent. His phone was never on before 9AM or after 5PM. He even made sexual advances to a couple of my female clients. Although being employed as a sales representative, I found myself running the day-to-day operations and dealing with overseas agents, clients and providers after hours as he was never reachable. We even lost a few clients that I had signed up, because he rudely fought with them. He was so paranoid that others were out to screw him, that he lost client's and my respect for him. Looking back, I am grateful to the universe that he was such a dreadful person as this gave me the opportunity to make a name for myself and make the key contacts that would soon be playing an important role in my life.

In April 2012, came the final turning point. My boss had this major argument with one of the clients named David. The argument was over the price of warehousing. He came back to a rate that we had agreed upon for this client, when he found out how much money the client was making. At the heart of the argument, he stupidly told the client that if he did not like the service and the new price, he could take his cargo and go somewhere else. Which the client promptly did.

The next day, David came and picked up his pallets from our warehouse and cancelled all the bookings he had with us. I was not happy, as I was the one who brought David on board. But little did I know this would be his loss and my gain.

Two weeks later, I got a phone call from David, and this is how the conversation went:

David: Hey, what are you doing working for this terrible person?
Me: Man, I need a job. I am too old to quit and find another job. It would be hard for me at my age. You realize I am 54 years old. Right?
David: Do YOU realize that you are the heart and soul of this company? clients know only you, not him, as he is never available.
Me: really? Do you think so?
David: Yes, and I think you should start your own business.
Me: ha-ha, I don't know about that. I don't have the funds to start a business.
David: Why do you need funds upfront for? Work from home. You'd be surprised how many people would come to you.
Me: I need cash flow as I need to pay shipping line upfront. They don't give credit.
David: if that's what stopping you, I will give you all my business and pay you before the cargo is here, so you can pay the shipping line. Come on, you can do this…

That night I couldn't sleep. I kept thinking about David's words. I was going to have to get out of my comfort zone. I needed time to think about this properly.

As mum was very sick, I decided to go back to Mauritius to see her. So, I resigned from my job as I wasn't sure how long I would stay in Mauritius and flew back home. While I was away, I had time to think about David's suggestions. I was scared and very uncomfortable with that idea, especially being in my 50s. I can't be starting a business, could I? Should I? But the more I thought about it, the more something in me started to feel right about the idea, plus I had the support of David. What have I got to lose? Oh yes, nothing, I truly had nothing. No house, no money. It would take me a few sleepless nights but, in the end, I made the decision to go ahead. What could go wrong? I could always find a job somewhere if it did not work out.

I came back to Melbourne after 2 weeks and the very next day, I registered GE Forwarding and Consulting. Most people I knew told me I was crazy to start such a venture during a year of economic downturn and at my age. But I was determined to go ahead. I still needed money for some set up costs, like buying a computer, paying the accountant to register the company with the government etc... So, I borrowed some money from my sister in England, and I pawned my two precious chains, one of which was a present from my mother and the other from my daughters. My heart was pounding, but I started believing in myself and knew I would do well enough to get my chains back.

I began reaching out to people I knew and started negotiating with shipping lines for rates. All of them supported me, although my ex-boss was putting pressure on them not to quote me. When he learned that I was starting my own business, my old boss rang me and started telling me I betrayed him and that I had no right to start my own business and that I had lied to him about my mother being sick etc. I must say though, never once did I ever think of stealing any of his clients although I was the one who brought the majority of clients on board. He had already lost David so that was fine. But I never approached anyone else, as I knew he had a young family, and I did not want to hurt them. Although, a few months after I started the business some of his clients rang me having found out that I was not working at the old company anymore and would eventually give me their business. And the business grew by word of mouth, each satisfied customer would recommend me to their friends and contacts. The rest is, as we call it, history. 4 months later, I walked into the pawn shop and with tears of joy in my eyes, bought back my chains. They have not left my neck since that day.

This part of my life taught me that I was better than I believed I was. I had overlooked my own talent due to being in a comfort zone which I was unwilling to look beyond, until circumstances pushed me out of it. It is like learning to swim by getting thrown in the deep end. You either swim or you sink and believe me, the first step is the hardest, but once you take a few more steps, it gets easier.

For the first few years, I was a one-man band. Working night and day, eight days a week. Going to bed after midnight and getting up at 5 every day. No weekends. I needed to get the company established. I could not afford a computer system, so all my records for the first 2 years were on an "excel sheet", which I still have in my possession to this day to remind me of my path and to remind me that when there's a will there's a way.

In 2018, I decided that to truly be successful, I needed recognition internationally, so I registered my business as a company and changed the name from "GE Forwarding and Consulting" to "GE International Forwarding Pty. Ltd". I joined a few international freight forwarding networks, and my business started to really grow. I also started going overseas to conferences. I found myself in countries where I could never imagine visiting in my previous life. Countries in the four corners of the world. The only continent I have not been to so far is Antarctica. Hmm, one day… That year, I also welcomed my first employee, Sam. I had to learn how to let go of some of my functions. It was hard, but it had to be done if I wanted to work "on" the business, instead of just working "in" the business.

Today GE International Forwarding Pty Ltd has seven employees and is well regarded in more than five international networks. The company has contacts in over 180 cities in the world and doing business with companies in USA, China, India and South America.

Last year, 2023, my son Sebastien voiced his desire to come and work with me and this made me so happy for now I know this company will go on and will be my legacy.

When I look back from where I come from, I am proud of my achievement. Although I had many setbacks, I did not crumble, I started a business with no money, only my determination and the support of two very special people in my life. I often wonder if my parents would be proud of me. Whether my mum would prefer I had my own business than being a doctor or lawyer.

I hope my story will be inspiring to young people out there starting in the industry. I am successful today because of the decisions I made. I could have decided not to start this business, and my life would be so different today. I would not have done the things I did, not seen the places I have seen, not met some of the beautiful souls I have met. Despite what happens to you, you must always think of the positive. There is a silver lining to every cloud. As I say in the beginning, things may happen to you, but it is how you react to them that will impact your life. I could have done the same thing many people in my situation have done. I could have given into alcoholism and gambling and being a horrible person because life was not fair to me. But no, this is a downward spiral and can only bring disaster. Instead, I chose to keep going and hoping something good would come along. And it did. Comfort zone is a killer of progress. A lot of ventures and relationships fail because we get too comfortable and stop working on the relationship. We take things for granted.

Now, what about the future you say? I had never dreamed of owning my own business before. Circumstance and change made me decide to do so, and for a long time I did not have a vision. Simply because I was too busy working in the business. But now, things have changed, and my dream is to really become International by opening offices around the world. I have my sight on Thailand and Europe to start with. They are my five-year plan. I dream to see the GE International Forwarding logo on the side of trucks and other transport vehicles. I would like my company to be recognized around the world. And I know I can do it with the help of the friends I have made in the industry. I have the determination and the passion. I would love to leave my children and grandchildren a Company they would be proud of. If I had one regret, it would be not having started the business when I was younger. But maybe, it would not have turned out to be as exciting as this journey was. Some may say that everything happens for a reason. Maybe, but I still think that it is the decisions that I made that were the deciding factor in my life.

The End

Gilbert Ernest
Resilient Entrepreneur and Inspirational Speaker in Logistics and Entertainment

Gilbert Ernest is a **dynamic entrepreneur, speaker, author, coach**, and **accomplished singer** with an extraordinary journey of turning **setbacks into success.** With a career spanning **decades**, Gilbert's **positive mindset** and **resilient spirit** have led him to triumph in both **business** and **personal challenges**, making him a respected figure in the **logistics** and **entertainment industries.**

As a former **ANZDL Salesman of the Year** (1996, 1997, 1998) and recipient of the prestigious **World Who's Who Businessman of the Year Award** (2013), Gilbert has continuously demonstrated **excellence** in his field. He further cemented his legacy by receiving the **WWPC Living Legacy Award** in 2017 for his remarkable contributions to the **global logistics industry.**

Gilbert's passion extends beyond business, having organized the first-ever **shipping industry charity ball** in 2003, raising nearly **$100K** for the **Royal Children's Hospital.** His commitment to

giving back to the community continued through subsequent charity events in 2004 and 2005. With a **global presence**, Gilbert has performed at prestigious events in **Los Angeles**, **Bali**, **New Zealand**, and across **Australia**, captivating audiences with his unique talent for **singing**. His performances have garnered recognition from individuals and corporations worldwide, making him a beloved figure both on and off stage.

Having faced significant personal and professional **setbacks**, including losing a **six-figure salary job** and family, Gilbert rebuilt his life and business from the ground up. His **resilience**, combined with a relentless belief in himself, led him to establish and grow his own company while competing with **multinational corporations**. Notably, his ability to build **relationships** and deliver **results** helped him secure major clients, including a key account in the **USA**.

Gilbert's story is a testament to the power of **persistence**, **resilience**, and never giving up, as he continues to inspire others through his multifaceted career and **positive approach** to life.

Reach out to Gilbert: Gilbert Ernest gernest@geforwarding.com.au

Chapter 6

Derek Scarbrough

My story

erek Scarbrough- Chronicles of a restless mind and quest for self discovery:

What are you running from? What are you chasing?
These two questions have been the primary focus on my continuous quest into self-discovery and meaning. The answers require deep introspective work and really investing in yourself. The answers, when found are humbling, grounding and profound.

We are creatures of habit. Breaking habits requires a deep intentionality that eludes many people.

I have found most people can tell you what they don't like, what they don't want but really mapping out what they want to develop within themselves and defining what they want and creating a plan/vision to achieve it is much harder.

There is a saying I love which is to choose your hard. Empowering. It puts the emphasis on us to realize we always have a choice in our actions. We are not the victim.

Growing up in Fort Lauderdale, FL was a surreal experience. To say it is a party town is an understatement. Two seasons: hot and hotter. The majority of the population is self-absorbed with money, alcohol and drugs all over the place. There is a reason it is called fort liquor dale! I come from a family riddled with addicts on both sides of the lineage as far back as you could go. Parents, grandparents, great grandparents, uncles, nieces, nephews, etc. I was not at all spared from the likes of addiction as we will come to find out later in this chapter. I was spoiled. Lived in a country club, privileged, upbringing.

We were raised in a home right on the intercoastal in Lauderdale by the Sea. This was back in the era of Z kavarichi's, rebook pump shoes and when desktop computers were first brought to the world. I am the oldest of three siblings with a younger brother and sister. There is a certain privilege and responsibility that comes with being the oldest with siblings. Even at a young age I felt a profound desire to take care of my younger brother and sister that has only grown stronger through the years.

It is amazing how we can remember certain episodes from our past so vividly. It is as if your mind can transform back to those certain moments, and you can literally feel the energy that came with the moment as if you were re-living it. My dad is standing at the edge of the bed with me, my brother, sister all laying together early in the morning on Friday. My mom is standing behind him crying. I can immediately tell something is serious and not right.

My dad proceeds to tell us he is divorcing my mom, moving out of our house to an apartment down the street. Shock, fear and concern reign over me. Was I the reason? What did it all mean? Not easy for an 8-year-old to fully understand. We soon learned that my father had committed adultery with mom's best friend thus ruining both marriages. Immediately the world I had come to know and grow up with started to change. The entire community we had come to know, play sports with, went to school with all changed with this news as my best friend was indeed the son of the woman my dad has committed adultery with.

This was the 1980's in South Florida and for context it was the time cocaine exploded into the US market with Miami/ Fort Lauderdale being the gateway. My parents have been drinking, smoking and using cocaine to excess for the past several years. My dad wanted to finally stop partying and change his life and just did not seem as if my mom was able or wanted to change and removing the partying from her life.

This was a major inflection point in my life.

I remember the concern I had for my mom in watching her both in that moment hearing the news and the time immediately after. How I wanted to help her, to take her pain away. About a week later my mom pulled into our driveway and couldn't get out of the car. I rushed outside to help but even at 8 years old I quickly realize that she was not hurt but had rather done this to herself. She was drunk and couldn't function. It all started to make sense given the behaviour and demeanour I had seen from her in the past week. She was often confused, aloof, uninvolved and slow. The concern and empathy I had felt so deeply quickly turned to disgust, contempt, judgement and disappointment as this realization set in.

My heart had been broken for the first time in my life. It took me a long time to fully realize that is what had happened to me.

She had stopped cooking dinners, taking care of us and I learned independence at such a young age. Subconsciously I also learned how to put up a protective wall, a bubble of sorts that has shaped the rest of my life. I conditioned myself over time to not fully realize how to give or even receive love.

This has really affected me throughout all the relationships with women in my life. That protective wall was omnipresent. Intimacy is so uncomfortable to me. It was essentially the end of any kind of loving relationship I had with my mother.

I would routinely lock myself in my room and then climbed out my window to run to my dad's apartment. He was often now home so I found myself alone a lot and learned to cope on my own without the willingness to ask or seek out help. I continued to tell myself I was strong enough to handle things and strengthened the protective bubble around me.

When I reached 8th grade I was still very much into athletics. I broke my arm playing football. As I healed and the summer came my dad got a beautiful older girl to drive us around over the summer to our various events. Stephanie is someone I will never forget. She was exciting, smart and someone I was immediately drawn to that opened up an entirely new perspective for me. It was during our first summer together that cigarettes, drugs and alcohol were first introduced into my life. They took over. Sports or athletics were no longer the primary focus of my life. Instead, it was the experimenting and experiences of drugs and alcohol that captured all my focus and attention.

I went to an incredibly prestigious, expensive and private school called Pine Crest. I always managed to get good grades but my defiance to authority to started to really take shape. I was constantly hanging and partying with Stephanie and her friends all of which were 3-4 years ahead of me. I started racking up dozens of minor infractions until the principal had seen enough and I was expelled at the end of 9th grade.

It turned out to be a wonderful thing for me in that I gained an entirely new crew of friends through my high school years, continued to do well in school and even ended up with essentially a full years' worth of college credits while graduating high school.

As I reflect on this time it is really amazing that I am still alive. I was drinking and driving DAILY. I crashed three cars, one of which before I was even legally allowed to drive and fled the scene! We were as wild as wild could be doing drugs before school, during school, after school and every weekend there would be a party at someone's house whose parents were out of town. Our favourite spot was a Polynesian restaurant/ bar called the MAI KAI. At 15 years old we would all have fake ID's saying we were 21 so we could go their bar and drink. They served a drink called "rum barrels" which were so strong you were only allowed to have two in any given night.

Throughout all this the "warning signs' of my behaviour were everywhere but my parents were aloof. My mom was off doing her own partying, and we would routinely use her house for all my friends to get together and party, so she was also complicit. My dad had turned to religion. He became a born again Christian and over time was indeed able to start partying.

I would split time between them using each of them for what I needed or wanted and then moving to the other. It started getting too difficult for me. All my dad would have had to do was look in my closest or even in my cars to see evidence of my usage, yet he never did.

Not only was I using drugs, but I was also selling them. I remember going to school as a 17-year junior in high school with 500 "roofies" in my pocket and selling them all. This was before they were considered the "date rape" drug as we would all routinely use them at parties each weekend.

Despite all the partying I was able to get a full academic scholarship to the University of Florida. I got an offer to be a roommate with a few guys that I had known growing up as a child playing sports with that were all part of the original community prior to my parents' divorce that I had really never spent time with after that.

I remember feeling uneasy about it as they were all athletic guys who did not and had not been living the party lifestyle that I had over our high school tenure. Despite the concern I decided to accept their offer and be their roommate. In all there were eight of us renting 2 apartments with four bedrooms/bathrooms right next to each other.

I will never forget packing and driving up to start my college experience. I was with my brother and the two of us were partying the entire way up to Gainesville, FL and stopped in Orlando for a few nights to see some friends. As we pulled in Gainesville and met everyone in our new apartments, I realized that I was the only one of the eight that did not have my parents with me. All the other parents were there moving in their children with pride and excitement. I remember feeling so unimportant and lonely in that moment that my parents didn't seem to consider my moving out of the house and going to college significant enough to merit their attention, concern or involvement. That bubble and contempt just building and building through time.

What a blessing it turned out to be to live in this environment! My friends would drink but overall were all healthy, going to the gym regularly and good influences.

I didn't realize it but looking back this time in my life would serve as a major turning point as it introduced me to the gym and to fitness which to this day is a non-negotiable in my life. I love the clarity and impact the non-negotiables in our life carry.

Wayne Hubers was a guy I had not known but who ultimately changed my life forever and for whom I will be eternally grateful. Never underestimate the impact you can have on other people! Wayne all but forced me to go to the gym with him. He was in very good shape. I remember how much I resisted but he was persistent. Wayne was so patient and willing to teach and show me everything.

I felt much less awkward in the gym knowing I was with him as he commanded respect by his demeanour, physique. I got an amazing trainer and friend. I started to go the gym with Wayne every day. I can never forget this gym. It was called Gainesville gym. It was OLD, DIRTY and rough. In a rough part of town. It was very cheap to join and get a membership. After the end of my first year at the University of Florida I had put on 15 lbs of muscle. I remember going back to my hometown of Fort Lauderdale for winter/Christmas break and all the comments from my old friends who couldn't believe I was the same person.

I was a Global Business major at the University of Florida. This was filled with all your standard business classes, but one feature of this major was that you were required to take a semester abroad. I was really excited about that. The college level credits I obtained in high school had me on a trajectory to graduate college in three years which I was able to ultimately do.

Everyone always asks me "why would you want to do that?" and the answer was always this desire to move to the next thing in life and restless urgency I have known throughout my life. The collegiate experience at the University of Florida was unique. The business school was so big they broadcast most of the classes on TV and on the internet. The classrooms were simply not large enough to hold all the students in each class. Professors became quasi celebrities as you would see them walking around campus. I had relied a bit on the teacher relationships in my life through High School always being close to them given the absence of my parents, so I wasn't a big fan of this set up at the University of Florida as it all but took away the personal touch and relationship with the teachers. What would typically happen is that you would know when each class would give their examinations, and you would end up watching 10+ hours of classes 1-2 days prior to the exam to "cram" for the examination. It also allowed for you to not have to be physical present at the university and still take the classes which did open up a few interesting things for me. I had started a relationship with a woman I could never forget, Arielle Molinet. She was the first real love of my life. She went to Tulane University in New Orleans which was about a 7-hour drive.

I ended up spending over a month in New Orleans in the middle of a semester at the University of Florida. New Orleans is an amazingly unique town. Along with San Francisco and New York City I would say as the most unique cities/towns in the USA. I had the chance to experience Mardi Gras. A massive carnival full of parades and absolute debauchery. Drinking, partying, drugs for what feels like two weeks straight. Just a WILD time and something that even during my partying days was enough to do just once. Arielle was the first woman who ever had that kind of influence on me where I was just captivated by her mind, her thoughts and her movements. She loved booked and turned me on to reading at a level I had not previously known. She had me reading Ayn Rand's The Fountainhead and Altas Shrugged. Both amazing books I highly recommend to this day.

I remember sitting in the courtyard at the University of Florida as I finished The Fountainhead. The sense of accomplishment in finishing a + 1000-page novel is real. As was the pattern in my life all the things I originally loved about Arielle would be some of the same things that I grew discontent for with the impenetrable bubble I had subconsciously grown around me and would eventually fall out of love with her.

My days at the University of Florida as a global business major progressed, I could hardly contain myself in going through the process of which country / city I would pick for my required semester abroad. My first choice was Helsinki, Finland but it ended up being full, so I went to my second choice of Madrid, Spain!

There was the problem of money. I had been working at Smoothie King near campus but going to Spain would require more money that I had. About eight months before going, I made a bold and risky decision to fund this trip that was going back to my upbringing and decided to sell pot / weed to help get the money for the trip. I went down to south Florida picked up 1 lb of pot and drove it back up to Gainesville and the University of Florida. I enlisted the help of one my high school friends who was also going to the University of Florida, and we began selling the drugs. I would proceed to do this trip back to south Florida 8 more times in the course of six months. I ended up selling the car and several of the possessions I had to finally be ready for my semester in Madrid.

I had conveniently left this semester abroad in Madid as my last semester needed to graduate college. What a way to go out! Live in Madrid for 4 months! Travel around Spain, Europe and go there knowing no one! What an adventure it would be! It was a BOLD move. I love BOLD moves in life. I have a track record of making them on grand levels and it is the excitement of the adventure and the unknown outcome that shapes it that riddles me with excitement to experience life! I had never travelled abroad but this burning desire for travel, experiences and exploring was DEEP inside me. I remember the feeling as if it was yesterday!

Before leaving, I was sitting down in Fort Lauderdale with my dad, and he asked me what I was going to do after I graduated and after this semester in Madrid. I honestly had no clue. He mentioned to me that his brother, Roger, was in some kind of business that was in some way related to Global Business (my major). Roger was coming down to Fort Lauderdale to visit, and we made plans to talk. He explained to me he was an international freight forwarder and his business was logistics. Funny enough, after three years as a global business major, I really had very little knowledge of this industry! Roger had started Scarbrough International, based in Kansas City, MO, 20 years prior. He was willing to give me a job, and I accepted. The plan was set that I would start with him and Scarbrough

International after my semester abroad in Madrid. I would move to Kansas City!

Trust me when I tell you this too was a BOLD decision; if you were from Fort Lauderdale, FL, your entire life, Kansas City is an altogether different place. Yes, they speak the same language, but that is about all that is the same. I even made plans to go visit him and see the office the week before going to Madrid and would ultimately leave from KC on my journey to Madrid.

Roger, at the time, was President of United Shipping Network. After spending a week in Kansas City with him, he also was introducing me to his partners in Europe that I would eventually get the chance to visit on my travels, which turned out to be quite special! That was my inception into the world of logistics in agreeing to work for him and start with Scarbrough International upon my return!

I took the flight from Kansas City to Chicago, where I had a long layover. I had managed to sneak a joint with me and went outside the Chicago airport while on my layover and remember smoking it while listening to my rap music, imagining all the possibilities of what was to come as I embarked on this great journey for my life.

The experience in Madrid was life-altering. I had been turned on to Jack Kerouac and started to read On the Road, which to this day is my all-time favourite book. Subsequently, I read most of what Kerouac ever wrote, but that was a perfect moment to be reading about the journeys he took as I experienced new people, countries, and languages. I was never the same. My love for cultures and travel will forever remain a part of my soul.

Living in Spain, I went to Saint Louis University, and they put all the students from abroad in local homes, typically with divorced women in Spain. It was there I met so many people, including a group that is very special to me to this very day. We called ourselves the "Conquistadores," and we drove through Spain together, slept on the beach in Cadiz, crossed into Morocco, went through Gibraltar, and spent months together. None of us had ever met until we got to Spain. We were from all over: the Midwest, the South, the East Coast, but shared this time and bond together that no one can ever take away. Since our time in Spain, we have met every single year together for at least one weekend in what is now 23 years running! A few years ago, we returned to Saint Louis University for our 20-year reunion.

I was able to travel on my own for several weeks, and it was one of the most defining experiences of my life. Taking trains throughout Europe, visiting Amsterdam, Hamburg, Switzerland, and France. Staying in hostels, reading, and meeting new people. I remember always being fascinated by how outgoing it helped me to become. No friends, no one to rely on, no one to tell you when to eat, sleep, etc. just me and the road. I grew up on this trip. I really did open up to put myself out there and be more available to strike up conversations and have an authentic curiosity. That is such an important aspect of life to me: curiosity. I have found many people have it at varying degrees, but acting on it, utilizing it for creativity and relationship building, and for deeper understanding still eludes most.

As the time in Spain came to an end, I was anxious to get back to the USA and start my career. I had been fortunate enough to meet some of the agents in Spain, Germany, and Switzerland from United Shipping. After all the traveling in Europe, I was more equipped for the permanent move to Kansas City. I would live with Roger and his family for the first several months in a small town of Kearny, MO, population 10,000. Such a massive change from anything I had known.

The plan was that I would start by learning imports into the USA and prepare to take my customs broker examination, which is offered twice a year in the USA. A four-hour test, open book, and much more based on time management and interpretation, knowing where to find the answers. Typically, only 20% of the people who take the test each time pass. I owe my education in logistics to Roger and his team. All too often, and no matter where your journey takes you, it is easy to lose sight of recognizing those that helped you along the way and made it possible for you. I was so blessed to have the opportunity to live with him, get the expedited learning curve, and exposure that most people that go into any job simply don't experience.

I was like a sponge. I wanted and needed to understand how everything worked from A to Z. Which parties were involved, why, how, and where did the opportunity exist? That same curiosity was coming out. Now, I will tell you that I am not the easiest person in the world to deal with when learning something I don't understand. I have that restless urgency to understand that permeates throughout the learning experience, which could be described as difficult until it clicks! I am proud to say that I maintain relationships with several people that were a part of helping to educate me in the very beginning, and they will forever be near and dear to my heart for not just what they did in educating me, but in the way they did it. That is something that is missed all too often in this world. It is not just what you do but it is how you do it. Character is a loaded word, but you know it when you see it. The trouble is, in my opinion, we don't see enough of it in the world these days.

I remember going to the first agent conference of my career: the United Shipping conference in none other than Fort Lauderdale, FL (my hometown). I was hooked. The chance to be in a room with people from different nationalities and cultures around the world, all in one exotic place, and spend time on the connections—learning about them personally (which to me will always be the most important), about their companies, and business. When you really stop to think about it, even to this day, it is one of the most amazing experiences and opportunities to have these conferences. Most people do not have the opportunity to experience such things in their life.

Eventually, I would move into my own little place, which was a small shared rented room near The Plaza (Kansas City's nicest area). It was the first time in my life I made an income. I bought a car and started to learn financial independence from my parents. That is a big moment in any person's life when you feel empowered. I remember that feeling and how it shaped my confidence.

My second cousin Sean also worked at Scarbrough International and became my direct boss. I remember so vividly a meeting I was pulled into with Sean and Roger. They asked me to consider NOT taking the customs brokerage examination in April (about four months into my employment at Scarbrough International), as they felt I was not studying and was unprepared. They also were extremely concerned about the optics of a "Scarbrough" not passing the test. Both Roger and Sean were licensed customs brokers. As much as I love them, this was a big turn-off to me and felt more ego-driven, which is not the way I ever want to live my life. Initially, I was quite mad, but that quickly morphed into motivation. Motivation is such a beautiful thing. No matter how it finds you, when motivation takes over, it can drive extraordinary focus and results. The key is to recognize the sign and embrace it when it hits, to lean into it and let it take over, and never ever ignore the blessing of motivation when it finds you!

I have vivid memories of Friday and Saturday nights studying instead of going out drinking and partying, which at this time in my life I still considered a large sacrifice. Sacrifice is so underrated. It is often what drives growth and success.

As I was studying for the test and learning import operations, the plan for me to go run their St. Louis office was in full effect. At the time, the office was a small office with three team members, dominated by one large export account of pet food that shipped from the USA all over the world. Maybe it made a little money, lost a little money, or broke even, but my mission was to grow the operation.

Driving into St. Louis for the first time with my uncle, I will never forget seeing the famed St. Louis arch in the window as we drove seemingly right into it. I felt like it was a rite of passage for me. This new city of St. Louis and the opportunity I had in front of me to make it a winner. I was riddled with anticipation, and the excitement consumed me.

It wasn't long until I got the news that I had passed the customs broker examination! The sense of accomplishment that comes with a result after deep sacrifice is as rewarding a feeling as there is. It gave me validation from my uncle, the leadership team, and the entire company. I didn't know the first thing about being a US Customs Broker. I knew how to take a test and was blessed that I didn't have years of experience under my belt and was fresh out of college. All were advantages.

Alas, the day came when I officially moved to St. Louis to take over the office. I was met with a lot of uncertainty by the three women team in place upon my arrival. They were experienced, tenured, and here was a 21-year-old nephew of the owner coming in to lead. They were really feeling me out to see how I would handle the situation. This was my first true beginning into leadership. Leadership is one of those loaded words. There are characteristics that can describe it, but it requires courage, humility, passion, enthusiasm, and connection to really achieve. You know it when you see it, and it can, and often does, have a drastic impact on lives.

I was excited to LEARN from the team there. To me, that is one of the first and most important aspects of leadership and a new mission: learn about it, immerse yourself in what and how the current operation is doing. Be willing to get on the front line to earn the respect of those involved before trying to change anything.

We had a small warehouse of about 2000 square feet that had not seen a piece of freight in a long time and was filled with files and breakroom tables and chairs. It was my first true exposure to a warehouse environment. I am not what you would call a handy man. I can't change a tire, and it would even be fair to call me a bit of a metrosexual. Learning warehouse operations would be another tough challenge and learning opportunity for me.

The first hire I ever made in St. Louis was a gentleman by the name of Aaron Hoorman. I owe a lot to Aaron. He was young, experienced, and taught me a lot. He had intimate knowledge of the St. Louis marketplace, had skills in the warehouse, and taught me how to build a pallet, shrink-wrap, use a forklift, load, and unload trucks. He is someone that I will always remember for the impact he had on my career and my life.

Aaron introduced me to others he knew in the industry, and slowly but surely, we filled up the warehouse and were able to maximize our opportunities as we grew the office. It was then that Patricia Dillon came into my life. She was a salesperson previously in pharmaceutical sales and started with us knowing very little, if any, about logistics, but she knew sales. Recollecting on this, it is quite telling that true salespeople are a different breed, and while knowledge of anything you are selling to some degree is always important and needed, it doesn't replace the tenacity and knowing how to build trust and gain business. In a service industry, at the end of the day, it is after all what people value most, and the best way to make pricing not the deciding factor is to establish trust.

I was blessed to get the chance to go on sales calls with Patricia and learn from her. She was so forthcoming and willing to share with me and really let me in. We made a hell of a team. With her support, we continued to grow the office until we had 25+ people in the office in three years.

Roger really gave me space and autonomy to run. Looking back, that was his leadership to me. He was reading me right in that I needed that autonomy to thrive. I often ask myself what my "why" was during this period…what was I chasing? The answer was really his approval. I was really doing it as much for him as for myself, and that is never the best way. My own ego started to show up thinking about the future and that "I could do this better." My relationship with Sean had started to deteriorate a bit as well. His leadership style was much different than I needed and wanted, and I had found it increasingly difficult to appreciate. I had a few conversations in passing and often when partying or altered with Roger about it and that I might need to move on and consider a different path. I don't think he ever took me seriously or fully remembered those conversations.

I started to recognize my own desire to take the knowledge I had gained and try to go start something on my own. I was 24 years old with the opportunity to make close to six figures, but it was the leadership style and direction of the company coupled with my ambition to stake my own claim that helped me finalize the decision to leave. It was emotional and hard. I wanted to do it right, so I drove to Kansas City over the weekend to have the tough conversation. Shock fell upon my aunt and uncle. That should never be the case if the relationship (which takes both sides) is in a good place. I offered to give them several months and as much time as needed, as I wanted it to be high level. Never burn bridges. That is something that was instilled in me at a young age and something I carried with me throughout my life. I told Roger that I wanted to open up my own company in Los Angeles.

I drove back and got a surprising call the next day on Sunday asking me to drive back to Kansas City on Monday morning for an exit interview and planning with Sean. I reluctantly agreed, as it is a good 3.5-hour drive each way.

Monday proved to be an overall very tough day. In talking with Sean in Kansas City, it was clear that the customers and clients belonged to Scarbrough International, and I was to return the laptop and equipment ASAP. I was honest with them that I did plan to tell the world where I was going and that I was opening up in a completely separate and different market, but that I didn't entirely agree that the customers "belonged" to them. However, I had no real desire to attack their clients and did have one main client that I had brought in as what was my first big and true sale that I did expect to follow me. I learned a lot during this, as oftentimes it is not just what you do but HOW you do it. I remember a quote that has always stayed with me: people put so much time into the beginning of a relationship but so little time in the end or to a separation. Separations have a lot involved in them and can be very difficult to navigate.

Undenounced to me, while I was driving to back to Kansas City on Monday my aunt Jeannie had driven to St. Louis to break the news to the team there. I only learned this upon driving back to St. Louis and going to the office to find it locked and being told I was no longer allowed in. They felt it was important to spin the separation in a way that allowed them to control the narrative and presentation to the St. Louis office. I can certainly understand that but again wish the HOW it was done was much different as that end play to our separation always alienated me.

The planning for GLC started in the fall / winter of 2005. I had just turned 25 and had saved $20,000 USD. I was ready to risk it all. The U-Haul was packed, and I rented a 1200 sq. ft apartment in Long Beach, CA on the beach that I had only seen pictures of but never seen in person. I was towing my car behind the U-Haul and will never forget that drive. My restless mind was in full swing. Figure out the moves, imagining the possibilities, visualize the success.

I pulled into my new apartment with the U-Haul, towing my car to see and old man with long white hair who looked at me as if I must be in the wrong place. He turned out to be my neighbour and became GLC's first ever courier shuffling documents all over town and in some cases even picking up agents and shuffling them to/from the airport. Whatever I needed he was there to support.

I started working out of my apartment. Things didn't go to plan. I quickly realized that despite registering the corporation I did not have a "corporate" customs broker license and only an individual license. This caused the first of what has now been tens if not hundreds of thousands of pivots required of most business and most entrepreneurs.

I would walk down to Long Beach customs facility daily to submit hard copy entries as this was before the fully digital environment. I would work and grind morning and nights, long hours. I would go down to airport customers and wait in line so many nights waiting for the customs officials to clear the cargo as you waited. I quickly realized the sacrifice this would take when I had gotten a personal effects shipment to clear and deliver to Pasadena, CA.

The client was urgent for it, and I was going to deliver it in my car to his residence! It happened to be ready and needed the night of a national championship game for my beloved college team of the Florida Gators. I didn't watch the game which for me was a HUGE sacrifice to deliver the cargo to the client!

The first shipment I ever secured was from an agent in Australia called Ambassador International. The history of GLC started with agent business and support. It just continues the theme of the power of relationships. I was so blessed to have gone to 10 different overseas conferences and build relationships that once again I completely and entirely owed to Roger and Scarbrough International for the opportunity to represent them at conferences.

I worked for six months out of my apartment. Had basically exhausted all my $ and things were tight. I had secured for my first nomination of 5 containers from China and quickly realized the next struggle that continues to be a struggle today in this business which is cash flow! I exhausted everything I had to pay the ocean freight, bill the client and then waited for their payment. Finally, the payment comes, I rush to the bank to deposit the check, and they tell me that since I am a new account, and the check is an out of state check they will have to "hold" the funds. I remember my outrage and overall inexperience with banks and often recall this memory with a smile mainly due to my own naivety.

As things progressed and being in Los Angeles I quickly realized that the market for warehouse and distribution was unlike anything I had ever seen. Driving by the port of Los Angeles for the first time was a similar feeling to seeing that St. Louis arch for the first time. A surreal moment that felt like a rite of passage as I tried to make it in this land. Again, I reflect back into my "why" or what I was chasing at this time, and I really think I was chasing validation. Can I make it on my own? Can I make it a place like Los Angeles with is the 4th largest port in the world saturated with competition.

I found a warehouse dispatcher office inside of a large existing warehouse facility in Carson, CA. I had a few docks over by the dispatch office that were not "mine" but were also not busy and began to promote warehousing services.

One new opportunity that came through was selling notebook planners to college universities. They had a container coming in and needed it to be unloaded so they could come load a U-Haul and deliver it to the universities just in time before the order and colleges cancelled the order. I unloaded the container, palletized it for them and help load it up and they got the freight to the colleges in time! I am proud to say that client is a still a client today and has grown their business significantly over the years.

Solutions, which is what logistics is all about. I often refer to a line I heard from my uncle Roger while on a sales call with him. So many things stand out to me about that sales call in that it was an existing relationship he had that had moved on to a new company (relationships matter, no burned bridges) and Roger said very correctly: "If you ship internationally, you will have problems. It is about the partner you choose and how the partnership together solves those problems that leads to success"

Remembering the experiences and lessons you learned along the way and paying that forward is what life is all about.

This was such a wonderful time in my life. I was 25, living in Los Angeles, started a company, seeing the opportunities come to fruition, low overhead, everything was new and exciting, and I was able to travel the world. I was partying HARD yet so focused and full of that youthful energy and spirit that hopefully never dies in any of us, ever.

Continued the grind and soon moved into our first warehouse building in Gardena, CA. 2500 sq. Ft, 2 dock doors but it was all ours.

Got involved with an international internship program that helped college graduates outside the USA come on a work visa for a year or a year and half to learn the business. What could be better for an international business? Carlos Moreno from Guatemala was the first guy I ever hired from GLC. Someone I can never forget. He shared the energy and passion for growth and learning. He helped get us off the ground and was willing to do whatever it took for us to grow. It didn't matter if it was in his job description. Anything that needed help, attention, support was his job description. How could I not love that as it has an entrepreneurial feel to it just thinking about it.

I would routinely make the deposits at our bank and had a teller who would help me often that I got to know. One thing led to another and Jeff Do came to join GLC! Never underestimate the people you meet as opportunities are all around us each and every day. He is someone who will forever be special to me. He too was willing to do whatever it took for us to grow. I have learned so many lessons in my journey, including many along these lines that are very recent, but building a team and keeping connected to them is one of the hardest things to do. Total authenticity in those relationships is critical to success. If you think about it relationships are tough. There isn't a relationship we have in our lives that doesn't meet challenge or conflict. Your brother, sister, parents, aunts, uncles, nieces, nephews, etc. All come with conflict. It is how we work through the conflict that ultimately determines the health and path of the relationship.

Slowly but surely, we continued to grow expanding into the

building next to us in Los Angeles. I reached out to another very important relationship in my life in Rodney Deneseus. I first met Rodney at United Shipping conference as one of the other younger guys there who immediately made it a point to make me feel comfortable, introduce himself and show that curiosity about my story. People can always sense that genuine curiosity. Rodney was another one who always showed up for me in a positive way. I convinced him to start a Chicago office out of his apartment in Schaumburg. We soon moved to a small office inside an existing warehouse in Chicagoland area using a page out of the playbook we had seen work for us in Los Angeles.

This was the start of additional offices and facilities. One of the biggest challenges in both my professional and personal career is not taking the time to appreciate accomplishments. It is part of that restless mindset. Scarcity vs. Abundance at odds with each other. As I am now 23+ years into my career in logistics I am still working on this balance professionally and feel further along personally toward a gratitude mindset of abundance.

All this time growing the company, traveling internationally, partying I had maintained plenty of relationships with women, but most were escapes. Long distance relationships that didn't demand more time that I wanted to give allowing me to concentrate on my career first.

As I hit 34 years old my family, desperate for me to slow down, with both my brother and sister already having marriages and children got me a match.com subscription which is an online dating platform. We had fun putting together my profile. The very first date I went on turned out to become my wife!

We met and fell in love so quickly and were pregnant within three months. When I think about our relationship it reminds me that we are all products of our upbringing. We all have traumas from our life, and some are more exposed than others. Some people are more a tune to their trauma's than others and we certainly all cope with them in our own ways.

The day I became a father, and my first-born daughter Jaselle was born was the day I was reborn. Of course, I knew being a parent would be a big deal, but I underestimated the impact it would come to have on me and my life. Driving home from the hospital with her in a tiny baby seat with my wife in the back seat looking back every millisecond to make sure she was ok I realized what real love is. Getting home and having NO idea what exactly to do and the wonderous adventure of raising a child has been the greatest adventure of my life. I have always been somewhat self-aware and would have describe myself as selfish. I felt significantly more self-less looking at my baby girl.

You would think in reading this that the experience of being a father helped remove some of my partying habits or at least calmed them down. The opposite happened.

It is 6am in Long Beach, CA and I am starting down at two huge lines of cocaine. I take them down. I proceed to move into the living room to take Jaselle downstairs for a walk. I am starting down at her while we walk, smoking a cigarette. It is a memory that will forever both haunt and guide me.

Funny what depths we can go to numb the pain in our lives. I was a full-blown addict at this stage in my life not going a day without being altered in some form or fashion. All the while I convinced myself that I could stop at any time…I still did my work, I still went to the gym. Inside I was broken. Was spinning from unhealthy things all around me with no vision.

Worse yet my wife who was calling out for my attention and who wanted nothing more than love and to be there with her found me distant, uninterested and often times combative.

Drugs are done in the dark. You often want to be alone, isolated or with other people who are doing the drugs. Misery, as they say, loves company. That was really it, I was miserable. In all kinds of pain. Years of masking the pain with substances. The mind is a very powerful thing. We can really convince ourselves of anything but in the end, we always know the honest truth even if we have blinders on believing the stories we tell ourselves. In the end that is really it isn't it? The story we tell ourselves. That shapes mindset which shapes actions which shapes behaviours which shape character.

I believe in divine intervention—moments and events in life that occur, after which, we are never the same. It was after a three-day "strategy" summit with our leadership team in Lake Tahoe, CA. All it really was, was an excuse to get together, party, and avoid home life. I drove my team back to the Reno airport while snow was dumping hard. I was living in Santa Cruz, CA, at the time, planning to drive home to my family, with my wife pregnant with our second child. While en route, the snow began to come down so hard that the police shut down the highway. I was forced off the road, and my car got stuck in the snow. There I was, alone, stuck, 2 am, drinking and smoking in my car when I got a glimpse of myself in the mirror, and the miracle happened. It was an epiphany—a flash of light and clarity so bright that I couldn't run away. I hated what I saw. Finally, my disgust for myself had reached the breaking point.

In that moment, I realized the strength to face my biggest fear, and that the partying, which was supposed to be "fun," had not been "fun" for a long, long time. I made the commitment to myself and to God right then and there to surrender. The calling for me to maximize my potential and help others was the strongest and clearest calling I had ever received. Strength and courage to change your life. I have met so many people that talk about change, but the action struggles to follow. I love big, bold moves!

I got sober from that moment and have never looked back—seven years at the time of writing this. Let's be clear: life didn't all of a sudden just get easier. I did begin to learn the tools to deal with it better and started a journey into self-discovery that is now a passion (some could say obsession). I have found that so many people can tell you what they don't want, don't like, and what isn't working, but very few can tell you what they really want or find and present solutions.

Another core result of my decision to get sober was re-evaluating where I wanted to spend my time. I had to rediscover what "fun" meant to me. Again, it came back to really thinking about what I want and what I like. It's very easy to fall into patterns—the infamous "comfort zone" that can prohibit growth and development.

Unhealthy relationships were much more easily identified. I now had the courage to remove them from my life. You have to appreciate how hard that is, as these are often friends, colleagues, and business partners—people and things you've known for years but now need to reshape or completely walk away from, depending on the circumstance.

Working out and going to the gym became a complete non-negotiable for me. Prioritizing my time took on newfound significance. There's a great line I think about all the time, and it still levels me: "Your standards are what you tolerate." Really think about that.

A life vision—I have thought a lot about this recently. What is it that I really want? Breaking the cycle of addiction in my family so that my kids and their children are keenly aware, educated, and led by example is a primary life vision for me. It means a lot to me that I have been sober for my youngest daughter, Jasmyn's, entire life. I insist on giving my children a different experience than I received from my parents growing up, mainly by being present and aware in their lives. I take that responsibility as a calling from God.

How do I live a life of service to help others struggling with addiction? You see, when you think about addiction, it's not just about one person. Addiction can ruin families. It can ruin lives.

It's not easy to ask for help. A great line I constantly remind myself of is that there is strength in needing others, not weakness. If you're out there and, however or whenever you receive this information, want a non-judgmental listener to support you, please reach out to me.

The confidence and mental strength that come with overcoming, with taking back control of yourself and your life, is a feeling that's hard to describe but changes you forever. I want to continue to highlight that this doesn't mean you figure everything out or that life gets easier.

I've had the most difficult time in my career over the past few years—the rise of the business during COVID and the resulting rightsizing that then occurred. I made the bold move to go for it, seeing where the industry was headed. Watching the rise was, of course, exciting. Opportunities were everywhere, but so was the chaos that followed, with steamship lines charging crazy fees for demurrage and per diem, months if not years after the fact. The residual damage was fairly severe, but so was the fallout when the business started dropping.

It forced us to make difficult decisions to right-size with the volume, and the easiest way to do that was by cutting salaries and team members. I never wanted to do it, and I failed to do it appropriately at first, delaying further action. A funny thing happened—everyone had great things to say about us during the rise, but the exact opposite during the fall. I learned many great lessons as a result, and finally addressed several unhealthy relationships that existed, but it was incredibly painful. The longer you tolerate things, the harder they become if not properly addressed.

Life is an adventure! To find our calling, our purpose, and to truly live is what makes us unique, and the experience special! More often than not, our true calling is not what we are currently doing, and finding the space and courage to recognize it—and act on it—is something special, magical when it happens.

I hear people talk about success all the time. What does success mean to you? For me, success means removing addictions, insecurities, and anxieties from my life, and living a life of gratitude, service, and adventure!

Addictions come in all forms. We live in a digital age—we're addicted to our phones, technology, work, overeating, and a host of other things.

I want to invite you on a journey of self-discovery. How can I love anyone else if I don't first love myself? How can I understand someone else if I don't first understand myself?

Peace. Peace of mind. These are things I now practice and pray for daily. Removing that restlessness is a constant challenge for me. I invite habits into my life that help, such as yoga, meditation, and giving myself permission *not* to always be active. I can't emphasize that one enough—**giving ourselves permission.**

Gratitude practices help as well, especially since my mind often gravitates toward thoughts like, *Why have I not reached a certain point?*

Why am I still in this position? What have I done wrong?—thoughts that don't serve me or anyone around me.

The practice of acceptance has been particularly hard for me to grasp. **Acceptance** and **surrender** tend to carry negative connotations, but they shouldn't. You are not giving up by surrendering—you are relinquishing. You are not allowing for below-average results by accepting—you are embracing where you are and allowing for improvement.

In the end, I am running from pain. I am chasing love. Knowing this has helped shape my character and blessed me with opportunities for growth. These are deep-seated and conditioned behaviours that are not solved quickly or easily. But I would ask you—what in life that's truly worth it is solved quickly or easily? **The beauty is in the work.** That's where transformation and growth happen.

What are you running from? What are you chasing?

The Logistics Legends

Derek Scarbrough
CEO | Supply Chain Management Specialist | Licensed U.S. Customs Broker
Location: Malvern, PA

With over 23 years of experience in supply chain management and logistics, Derek Scarbrough serves as the CEO of GLC Holdings, Inc. and TCA Staffing, Inc. His extensive expertise has positioned him as a leader in the industry, overseeing strategic operations and fostering growth through his passion for leadership and sales management.

Professional Achievements:

- Licensed United States Customs Broker
- Awarded 'Marketing Professional of the Year' in 2022 by the Marketing Association

Educational Background:
Derek holds a Bachelor's degree in Global Business from the University of Florida, further solidifying his foundation in global trade and management strategies.

Skills & Expertise:

- Leadership & Strategy
- Sales & Management
- Supply Chain Optimization

Personal Touch:
Seven years sober, Derek is passionate about fitness and outdoor activities, including biking, hiking, skiing, and running. He believes in living life openly and values transparent communication. His deep connection to nature and commitment to serving others fill his soul and drive his professional ethos.

Professional Affiliations & Community Involvement:

- Member of Entrepreneur Organization (EO)
- Active member of NCBFFA
- Member of WCA, GAA, GFK, WWPC, WFN, JC TRANS, OLO
- CTPAT Certified

Contact Information:

- **Email:** dscar@glc-inc.com
- **LinkedIn:** Derek Scarbrough | LinkedIn
- **Phone:** +1 562-221-3485
- **WeChat:** derekglc

Derek is a driven and transparent leader who brings a wealth of experience to the supply chain sector. Reach out to him for strategic insights and leadership in the world of logistics and beyond.

Chapter 7

DEEPANKER PARASHAR

My story

*E*arly Life – something I didn't like to remember much, but today I value its importance and roughness in more ways than one.

If I could go back in time, I would have said, "Let me warn you," but today, after 38 years, 5 months, and 17 days, my words have mellowed with a cocktail of wisdom earned through the years. Now, I would say, "I am happy to inform you today… You are all going to be the second people on this planet to know the crux and truth of my inner self."

I was born into a middle-class family in India, where values like hard work, perseverance, and education were emphasized from an early age. My parents, who worked tirelessly to provide for our family, instilled in me a sense of discipline and a thirst for knowledge.

However, since adolescence—1984 onwards—a uniform, especially the **pips on the shoulder**, fascinated me as a young boy. This isn't something extraordinary; I'm sure many have had similar fascinations, and some were lucky enough to follow theirs, turning them into lifelong engagements.

But my story during this time was not so rosy. In fact, **not so rosy at all**.

To add a pinch of context: our country, and more personally, our family, was going through a typical phase for a middle-class Hindu household. Most of the elders in our family were academics or engineers, with a modest monthly family income of around US$146. Needless to say, bills were always delayed and "to-be-paid" was a frequent phrase in our home.

I could keep going, as I remember these times vividly, with exact dates and instances, yet through it all, there was togetherness.

Cutting the long story short, this was an important phase of my boyhood. Despite the unorganized chaos, I was still looking forward to growing up and earning those **pips on my shoulders**.

Conversations with Dad:

In our family, back in those days, it was firmly believed that if you were a boy, you had to become either a doctor or an engineer. If you were a girl, your only option was to become a teacher. That's just how things were. My dad and I had many conversations—or should I say, **one-sided conversations**. He would talk, talk, and keep talking, while I would just listen, listen, and keep listening.

He wanted me to become a doctor, to prepare for and sit the MBBS exam, which typically required 2-3 years of preparation after high school. But I never had the passion for it. It took him three long years to realize that this was not the path for me. Unfortunately, by then, the tragedy was that I had missed the cut-off age for the entrance exam for the uniformed career I dreamed of—the **pips on the shoulder**.

I guess we never truly understood each other, and what should have been a real conversation—where he could guide me and I could listen, not just hear—never happened. (This is a life lesson I now use as a parent, to **listen** patiently, not just hear).

Life without Pips and the Uniform:

It was tough at that age and at that stage of my life. I was on a rollercoaster ride, propelled and pressured by the typical joint Hindu middle-class family virtues and stigmas. However, whether I knew it or not, this phase was teaching me **adaptability**, **optimism**, and how to focus on what's in front of you, rather than what's gone by.

Believe me, this is an amazing virtue. Over time, it started rebuilding my broken confidence and dismantling the disempowering beliefs I had. Slowly but surely, I gained the confidence to realize that there could be life without the uniform, and that success doesn't always have to come with pips on the shoulder.

And so, the next journey began...

Turning Points:

Switching from Science to Commerce—subjects like Biology, Botany, Anatomy, Chemistry, and Physics were now replaced by Business Accounting, Business Organization, Accountancy, Economics, and Statistics. This was where I began to truly believe in a couple of proverbs:

a) **Never say die**
b) **When life throws lemons, don't throw them back—instead, grab a glass of water, add a pinch of salt or sugar, make lemonade, and enjoy.**

Positivity was building within me, likely because I was learning to murder the inner fear and let go of past failures and setbacks. For the first two years, I had to burn the midnight oil as I transitioned from being a science student to studying commerce. But as they say, hard work pays off, and eventually, I graduated from Delhi University with a Bachelor of Commerce.

My First Summer Job:
I was 21, and she was 22!

Ah, before I get into my first summer job, let me set the context. It was Valentine's Day, 1993, and I was lucky enough to have found someone special. By this time, I was 21, and she was 22. We decided to meet up, but reality hit me hard—I didn't have any smart dating outfits. For the first time, I was truly disappointed by my financially limited background. Coming from a middle-class family with no real conversations with my dad, I was acutely aware of my lack of resources.

However, as you know, I had already embraced **optimism** and the **"never say die"** mentality. I was blessed with amazing friends who came to my rescue for this special occasion—my first date on Valentine's Day! Thanks to them, I had a pair of jeans, a bike, and a leather jacket. I even had enough pocket money for two Coca Colas.

But there was a nagging fear—**what if she asked for something more than a cola?** I had learned my lesson from childhood about "**to-be-paid**" bills, but luckily, she was happy with just one cola, and I was even happier that she didn't ask for anything more!

To this day, we still laugh about that moment—**LOL** as the kids say now.

My First Summer Job: The Leather Jacket
(Another Turning Point)

With a salary or stipend of US$29...

Fortunately—or unfortunately—my Valentine complimented me on **the** leather jacket (yes, **THE** Leather Jacket). She mentioned it looked good on me and said she would like me to wear it again on our next date. Naturally, being at that age and eager to impress (with a bit of inherent male pride), I couldn't admit that everything she was admiring was on loan for just four hours!

Now, imagine being a boy from a **Hindu middle-class joint family**, who didn't follow the expected path of becoming a doctor and who never had a real, two-sided conversation with his dad. How was I supposed to afford this jacket—or even find a way to finance it (ha ha)? This sparked something in me. I needed to find a solution.

Luckily, through word of mouth (remember, this was not the mobile phone era), I got a message to meet someone at their office. To my surprise, I was introduced to their boss, and she offered me a job starting the following Monday. And believe me, I was thrilled! Do you want to know why? **I was offered US$30!** That meant, after 30 days of doing this sales job, I could afford my second date with my Valentine, and more importantly, I could wear my own leather jacket this time!

Of course, I bought the jacket. It had already been earmarked for me months before.

As a cherry on top, the shop owner, seeing my commitment and devotion, gave me a discount of **US$7**, which meant I could even finance my next date! This time, I brought along my three friends—the bike owner, the jeans owner, and **the leather jacket owner**—and introduced them to my Valentine. We had a little more cash this time and could even afford snacks to go along with our colas. We were all **happy chappies**.

New Work Offer:

Not long after, my team leader from that summer job resigned to join another company. He relayed a message to me through a common connection, and we met at his new office. As they say, history repeats itself—he wanted me to meet his new team, and they offered me a new opportunity, a completely new product to sell, and a new learning curve for me.

Seeing the financial offer, I didn't hesitate. I said yes—and the rest is history.

This marked the **beginning of my journey in freight forwarding**.

A Journey Across Continents: 30 Years in the World of Logistics

As I've mentioned before, I was born into a middle-class family in India, where values like hard work, perseverance, and education were emphasized from an early age. My parents worked tirelessly to provide for our family, instilling in me a sense of discipline and a thirst for knowledge. This foundation became crucial as I pursued higher education and eventually embarked on a career in logistics and freight forwarding.

Being a commerce graduate, the world of logistics always fascinated me. During a university project, I became intrigued by the intricacies of how goods moved from one part of the world to another. This curiosity would shape my entire professional journey—a career that has now spanned over three decades, traversed continents, and evolved as the world around me transformed.

The Early Years: Finding My Path

After completing my MBA with a specialization in Marketing Management, I found myself at a crossroads. While many of my peers gravitated toward traditional corporate roles in finance or marketing, I felt a different pull. The world of logistics—complex, dynamic, and integral to global commerce—**called to me**. I realized that this field offered something unique: the chance to be part of a global system where every decision had the potential to impact markets worldwide.

Embarking on my career in logistics was not without challenges.

The industry was fast paced, demanding not only technical knowledge but also the ability to think on your feet and adapt to an ever-changing environment. Freight forwarding, in particular, was intricate, full of variables like regulations, customs, transportation networks, and unforeseen delays. But these challenges only fuelled my passion.

One thing that was crucial in both my early summer job and my new logistics career was the customer. I knew that the key to success, then and now, was building strong relationships. I believed—and still do—that I was a strong marketer, someone who valued clear, transparent communication and long-lasting relationships founded on honesty. I call it relationships for life.

Building Expertise: Learning from Global Experience

Over the years, my career took me across various geographies around the globe, offering invaluable insights into different cultures, economies, and business practices. I had the privilege of working in diverse regions, each presenting its unique set of challenges. From the bustling ports of Singapore, Malaysia, and Asia to the vast supply chain networks of Europe and the rapidly evolving markets of the Middle East, I witnessed firsthand how different countries approached the same logistical problems in vastly different ways.

In Singapore, Hong Kong, and Malaysia, I learned the importance of efficiency and speed. These regions were hubs of manufacturing and export, where meeting tight deadlines and managing complex supply chains were critical to success. Working closely with local teams, I came to respect their work culture, which prioritized precision and attention to detail. This experience taught me the value of blending local knowledge with global expertise.

Europe presented an entirely different set of challenges. The regulatory environment was stringent, with a strong emphasis on sustainability and innovation. Navigating the complexities of European Union regulations added layers of difficulty to freight forwarding, but it also sharpened my skills in regulatory compliance and problem-solving.

Africa, with its emerging markets, taught me resilience. The logistics networks were underdeveloped, and the transportation infrastructure was limited, but this presented opportunities for innovation. I worked closely with local stakeholders, building relationships and finding alternative routes to ensure goods reached their destinations, despite the many obstacles.

This exposure to different markets excited me. Each experience offered ahead-of-its-time insights, which I incorporated into my work, creating what I called innovative work fusions that I applied across various regions.

Returning to India: New Horizons and Challenges

After years abroad, I made the decision to return to India. It wasn't just about coming back to my roots, but also about contributing to the rapidly growing logistics sector in my home country. India was undergoing significant transformations with industrialization and an increasing focus on global trade, yet the logistics industry faced serious infrastructural challenges—poor road networks, fragmented supply chains, and inconsistent regulatory frameworks. Additionally, I wanted my children to receive a grassroots cultural education back home.

Armed with years of international experience, I saw an opportunity to help modernize logistics in India. I became involved in streamlining operations, implementing global best practices, and embracing technology to address some of the logistical challenges. One of the most significant changes I led was the adoption of digital logistics platforms, which improved visibility, enabled real-time shipment tracking, and optimized routes. These innovations not only enhanced efficiency but also reduced costs for businesses—a valuable lesson I'd learned from working with customers and vendors in Guangzhou, China.

At the same time, I had to navigate the complexities of Indian regulations and customs processes, which were notoriously slow and cumbersome. My experience in Europe and Southeast Asia, where I had learned to operate in highly regulated environments, proved invaluable here. Over time, my team and I developed processes that mitigated delays, ensuring that goods moved smoothly through the system.

Industry Challenges observed & lessons learnt:
Over the years, the logistics industry has faced its share of disruptions, from economic downturns to technological shifts. Perhaps the most significant challenge came with the global COVID-19 pandemic. The world came to a standstill, and global supply chains were thrown into chaos. Ships were stuck at ports, air freight was halted, and land transport became a logistical nightmare due to lockdowns.

For someone who had spent a lifetime working in logistics, it was both a challenging and eye-opening time. The pandemic underscored the importance of adaptability. It wasn't just about moving goods anymore; it was about ensuring essential supplies like medical equipment and vaccines reached the people who needed them most. My team and I worked round the clock, leveraging technology and our vast network of contacts to navigate the chaos. It was a test of everything we had learned over the years—the importance of quick decision-making, the value of trusted partnerships, and the need to remain resilient in the face of adversity.

This phase of pandemic also taught us the Work from Home Culture, as conventionally we never could have adopted the same in inherent old mindsets. I observed, if we empower our teams and develop trust and empathy towards all this not only brings operational costs lower, but also improves the efficiency and brings better results.

All work & No Play makes jack a dull boy. The Passion for Motorcycling: My Life Beyond Work

Remember from above, the uniform the pips the outdoor extravagant career …. a hint of same i share with you …

While logistics has been my professional calling, my personal passion has always been outdoor activities & motorcycling. There's something about the open road, the wind on your face, and the sense of freedom that comes with riding a motorcycle that's unparalleled. **For me, motorcycling is more than just a hobby—it's a form of meditation,** a way to clear my mind and find balance amidst the hectic demands of my work and act like a stress buster

I've been fortunate to explore various parts of the world, both on and off the job, and some of my most cherished memories are from my motorcycle journeys. Whether it was navigating the winding roads of the Himalayas or riding along the scenic coastal routes of Europe, these experiences have taught me lessons that I've applied to my professional life as well. **Riding a motorcycle requires focus, patience, and the ability to adapt to changing conditions—traits that have served me well in the logistics industry.**

In many ways, my passion for motorcycling has complemented my work in logistics. The thrill of exploration, the excitement of discovering new routes in other words getting past the fear of un-known and the satisfaction of overcoming challenges are common to both.

My take on this is: no matter how busy life gets, it's essential to find time for the things that make you feel alive, this is one of them for me.

Family: The Foundation of My Success

Though above we point-blankly discussed, me and my father always had a one-sided conversations specially science, commerce, uniform etc ... however, i feel the optimism developed through all this and the process of filtration an sedimentation or in my science language the litmus test in totality my father got convinced with the conviction he saw in me with constant professional & financial growth above all Happiness amongst the family. I am happy to say as stated above **USD$ 146** have gone past and we are all having Comic's blessings and having a good life yet all still as a Happy Hindu Joint family we stay with our senior parents aged 90 & 85 years respectively

Behind every successful professional journey is a strong support system, and for me, that has always been my family. My parents, now senior citizens, have been my pillars of strength throughout my life. Their hard work and dedication instilled in me the values that have guided me through my career. **Remember my Valentine …I'm blessed and proud to say she's My wife now,** with her deep spiritual grounding, has been my constant source of motivation and balance. Together, we've raised two wonderful boys, and they continue to inspire me every day, By the blessings & their hard work now they are working in Europe and improving there learning curve ... as exactly i did back in the days and still treasure those experiences & memories.

Balancing a demanding career with family life has not always been easy, especially when work required extensive travel and long hours.

But through it all, my family has been there for me, providing the support and encouragement I needed to keep going.

They've helped me maintain perspective, reminding me that while professional success is important, it's the relationships we build and the people we love that truly matter.

My Friendships for Life & Bonds

I am sure, you remember the bike, the jeans and the leather jacket how they made our Valentine feel good & the Leather Jacket giving me a turning point so on and so forth … …

Especially these three along few more we are obviously like a family know, with all our children having amongst theme there amazing friendship nurturing and growing, giving us the peep into how we all started three or even four decades before our life journey's ….

Throughout my life, one constant source of joy and stability has been the friendships I've cultivated. In particular, I'm fortunate to have a few friends from my school days with whom I share a deep and enduring bond. These are not just friendships born out of nostalgia; they have grown and evolved over the years, weathering the changes that life has thrown our way.

Our friendship has become an integral part of not just our lives but our families as well. We've shared countless memories—from childhood mischief to our early careers and beyond. As we've grown older, our families have become intertwined, and now our children know each other, continuing the tradition of closeness that we've fostered for decades. These friends are more than just companions; they are my extended family, a constant reminder of where I came from and the values that have shaped me.

Despite the demands of my global career, I've always made time to nurture these relationships. Whether it's gathering for a simple meal or planning trips together, these moments remind me of the importance of staying grounded. No matter how far I've travelled, I know I can always return to the comfort of these friendships, where I am understood not as a logistics professional or business leader, but simply as a friend.

Global Partners, Extended Family

As my career in logistics took me across continents, I had the privilege of working with partners and colleagues from all over the world.

What started as professional relationships gradually blossomed into friendships—deep connections that went beyond business deals and contracts. Over the years, many of these individuals have become more than just partners; they've become like family.

These global partnerships have been invaluable, not just from a business standpoint but on a personal level. Whether in Asia, Europe, or Africa, I've built relationships based on trust, mutual respect, and a shared commitment to excellence. I've spent countless hours working side by side with these partners, overcoming logistical challenges, navigating cultural differences, and celebrating successes. In time, we've celebrated not just business victories but also personal milestones—birthdays, weddings, and even holidays spent together.

For me, these global partners are not just people I work with; they're an integral part of my extended family. I've had the privilege of being welcomed into their homes, meeting their families, and sharing in their traditions. Likewise, when they visit India, I welcome them into my home, where our family's bond over shared meals and stories. These relationships have enriched my life in ways I never anticipated when I first entered the logistics industry.

The beauty of these global connections is that they remind me of the interconnectedness of our world. Despite the geographical distances and cultural differences, we share common values—trust, loyalty, and friendship. These partners have played a significant role in shaping my professional journey, and they continue to be a source of inspiration, support, and camaraderie.

A Heartfelt Gratitude: Honouring & Thanking people who matter in making -of -me.

Behind every success story there are always God sent representatives of influences and mentors, individuals who shape us, teach us, and inspire us in ways we sometimes don't fully realize until we reflect on our journey. For me, this starts at home, with my first teacher—my beautiful mother. She was my first guru, guiding me with love, wisdom, and resilience. Her quiet strength and unwavering belief in me formed the foundation of who I am today. My gratitude to her knows no bounds, as her lessons continue to guide me, both in my personal and professional life.

I extend my heartfelt gratitude to my grandparents and my father, who instilled in me the values of hard work, integrity, and humility. Their life lessons shaped my character and gave me the drive to succeed in a complex and challenging industry. They taught me the importance of staying grounded, no matter where life's journey takes me.

In my professional career, I owe thanks to the many ex-managers and bosses I've worked under. Each one taught me valuable lessons—some through guidance and mentorship, others through the challenges they presented. These individuals helped me build a solid foundation, providing both opportunities and wisdom that I continue to carry with me today.

However, I reserve special thanks for one senior, in particular. This individual always believed they were correct, though, in reality, they taught me some of the most profound lessons by showing me what not to do. It is often through witnessing mistakes that we learn the most, and in this case, I realized the importance of authenticity, humility, and careful decision-making. The lessons they unintentionally imparted have proven invaluable throughout my career, teaching me to approach situations with a balanced perspective.

I offer my deepest gratitude to a recent inspiration—an angel I had the privilege of meeting not long ago. This person has been a constant source of motivation, defying all expectations I had about where inspiration comes from. It's a humbling reminder that inspiration is not bound by age or experience; it can come from younger minds if we remain open to new ideas, willing to rethink, re-innovate, and reboot ourselves. She has shown me that life is an ongoing journey, one that should be approached with a mindset of limitless potential and unstoppable drive. In this world where the rules constantly change, the key to success is to play on a no-limit table, where adaptability and forward-thinking bring true victory—not just in business, but in life itself.

I am sure you all have not forgotten, however I will not let you forget, MY Valentine (remember the Leather jacket the first date) am honoured and blessed to say Now my Wife Enakshi, i would have not been what i am and who we are as a Family. thanks for standing through all weathers, seasons and rains and storms, ultimately making your spiritual, pure and unwavering beliefs making us all bind as a Bouquet of Love and Blessings!!

Remember: Our Beliefs shape our lives!!
Thanks for patient reading!

Deepanker Parashar
Founder & CEO, AADE Trans

Deepanker Parashar embarked on his **freight forwarding journey** on **July 21, 1994**, and has since dedicated **30 years** to mastering the **logistics industry**. A seasoned **freight forwarding professional** from **India**, Deepanker has honed his expertise across **Southeast Asia** and **Europe**, excelling in providing **innovative solutions** and **competitive pricing** for a wide range of **freight forwarding products** and their derivatives.

Known for his unwavering commitment to **strong PR** and **networking**, Deepanker seamlessly connects with people from **diverse global nationalities**. His values of **honesty** and **transparency** underpin every interaction, ensuring trust and clarity in his professional dealings. As the leader of **AADE Trans**, Deepanker is focused on strengthening the company's **Aviation** and **Pharma verticals** over the next **2-3 years**, having already established a solid foundation in these areas.

Beyond his professional pursuits, Deepanker is a **fun-loving** and **spiritual** individual who deeply respects **all religions** and **global**

cultures. His philosophy—"**Challenges are options and opportunities for growth**"—extends into his passion for **motorcycling**, where he lives by the motto, "**Straight roads never made skilful riders**." His career and personal life reflect an ongoing commitment to **learning**, **growth**, and the **pursuit of excellence**.

Starting as a **management trainee**, Deepanker has held various senior roles, including **Country Head**, before founding his own **startup**. Today, he leads **AADE Trans** with a vision of **global market expansion** and is actively seeking **partners** and **collaborations** to further that mission. At **AADE Trans**, the belief is simple: "**The world is our market**."

For inquiries, reach out to Deepanker Parashar at:
Email: dparashar@aadetrans.com

Chapter 8

Dr. Sri Rasamanickam

Dr Sri's story

Abstract

This is the story of an exemplary entrepreneur who built an empire in a foreign land. His success stands among the best in the world, having arrived in Switzerland as an immigrant from Sri Lanka. Forced to flee his homeland due to civil war in 1986, Sri Rasamanickam worked tirelessly to stabilize his life, eventually founding his own business and achieving success through sheer hard work, commitment, and determination. His resilience in the face of adversity allowed him to grow his global logistics business significantly. Rasamanickam carved a niche for his company in Switzerland's highly competitive business environment through customer-focused practices and transparent dealings. Coming from a war-torn nation, he established his global logistics business on solid fundamentals and a vision of consistent success. His life and remarkable business achievements in a foreign land are sure to inspire aspiring entrepreneurs, which is why his story is worth studying.

Background

Sri Rasamanickam was born in Jaffna, in the northern part of Sri Lanka. His father was a small-time entrepreneur involved in local trading, and his mother was a homemaker. Rasamanickam dreamed of becoming a mechanical engineer and enrolled in Jaffna Technical College to pursue his passion. However, fate had different plans. In 1989, at the age of 20, a brutal civil war forced him to flee Sri Lanka due to the escalating unrest. He arrived in Switzerland as an immigrant, unfamiliar with the culture, language, and business climate.

Upon arriving in Switzerland, Rasamanickam quickly realized the importance of learning German to integrate with the local community. He enrolled in a language course and learned German swiftly. He then worked in a restaurant for a year to save money and fund his education in Logistics Management—a decision that would shape his future as a respected entrepreneur.

Today, Rasamanickam enjoys a successful career with three companies in Switzerland, and he has no regrets. He is a happy family man with two children and his wife, Vasantharani, who also works as a director and CFO in his businesses. Known for his soft-spoken nature and eagerness to learn, Rasamanickam's continuous learning has contributed to his business success, keeping him aligned with industry trends. He regularly attends workshops and business networking events worldwide to expand his connections.

In addition to his business pursuits, Rasamanickam has political ambitions and is a member of the SP Party, a leading political party in Switzerland. He is nominated as their candidate for City Councilor in the upcoming election, with polls predicting a favorable outcome. Despite his busy schedule, he always finds time for his passions—travel and reading.

Short Introduction about Sri

Dr. Sri Rasamanickam's story is one of vision, determination, and global influence. With over 25 years of experience as a Global Logistics & Supply Chain Professional, he has led the growth and success of numerous organizations across culturally diverse environments worldwide.

Sri began his journey as the founder and CEO of Aero Lines GmbH, based at Zürich Airport in Switzerland, in 2004. Under his leadership, Aero Lines has grown into a leading freight forwarding and global logistics service provider, offering solutions that span the globe. His ability to craft and implement strategic business plans has been pivotal in driving sustainable, long-term growth with consistently strong financial outcomes.

"The best way to predict your future is to create it." Sri Rasamanickam is among an elite group of entrepreneurs who created their future and built a business empire in a foreign land from humble beginnings through effective leadership and smart application of knowledge. Like many successful businesspeople worldwide, he possesses a "die-hard" spirit that drives him to succeed despite numerous challenges. His ability to turn adversity into opportunity has brought success knocking at his door.

Forced to flee Sri Lanka at the age of 20 due to civil war, Rasamanickam left behind his studies in mechanical engineering and moved to Switzerland for survival. In this unfamiliar country, he took a job at a restaurant, saving his earnings to learn German and study Logistics Management. While many of his peers spent money on entertainment, food, and liquor, he invested in knowledge and skills.

Sri Rasamanickam's journey is one of resilience, courage, and unwavering determination. His story began with the joy and sense of achievement that came with being promoted to manager at

Zurich Airport. For Sri, it was a milestone—a moment that validated years of hard work. But in the blink of an eye, that triumph was shattered.

Within just one hour, he went from being someone to feeling like no one when the company he worked for suddenly announced its closure. The news hit hard—everything he had built seemed to vanish. He felt the weight of uncertainty not only for himself but for his colleagues who were facing unemployment. The emotions of that day still linger: the disbelief, the frustration, and the deep concern for those whose livelihoods were at stake.

But in the face of that adversity, Sri made a bold decision. Instead of succumbing to fear, he chose courage. Within 24 hours, he approached his manager and uttered the words that would change his life: "I want to buy the company." Though he had little capital and even less time to pull together the funds, his determination outweighed his doubts. His heart was set not just on saving his own career, but on protecting the jobs of those around him.

The next few weeks were filled with intense struggles—sleepless nights, countless meetings, and the anxiety of securing funding. He searched for solutions relentlessly, pushing through his fears. It wasn't easy. There were moments when the task seemed insurmountable, but Sri's desire to take care of his team drove him forward. His vision was clear: to not only keep the company afloat but to create a future for the people who relied on him.

Finally, after much effort and against all odds, Sri purchased the company. It was a moment of triumph, but also the beginning of a new challenge. Running Aero Lines GmbH was no easy feat. The initial days were difficult, filled with unexpected hurdles and learning curves.

But Sri's tenacity paid off. Slowly but surely, the business grew, and his efforts started to bear fruit.

Today, Aero Lines GmbH is thriving, handling consignments from 150 countries through a global network of associates and partners. Sri Rasamanickam's journey from a logistics manager to a company owner is a testament to his courage and commitment, not only to himself but to those who almost lost their jobs. His heart for his people and his unwavering belief in finding a way forward turned what seemed like a failure into a powerful success story.

He operates full-fledged offices in Switzerland, Sri Lanka, India, and Canada, employing over 100 people from diverse backgrounds. Despite starting with no knowledge of Swiss culture or language, Rasamanickam has achieved remarkable growth, employing people from various countries who speak languages such as French, German, Italian, Tamil, Turkish, Chinese, and Hindi.

Currently, he manages three companies and is planning to start a fourth in the England's, partnering with another entrepreneur. This new venture will focus on B2B services.

Sri's career is not only marked by his business acumen but also by his commitment to continuous learning and professional development. He holds certifications from prestigious institutions, including the IATA Training & Development Institute in Geneva and the Federal Office of Civil Aviation in Bern. His achievements have been recognized with a European Professional Doctorate from RUSHFORD Business School in Geneva and a Doctoral Diploma in Entrepreneurship, Strategic Leadership, and Innovation Management from MAVERICK Business Academy in London.

Beyond his professional achievements, Sri has also made significant contributions to his community through political involvement.

Since 2017, he has served as a member of the Election Commission in the City of Olten, Switzerland, and has been an active member of the Social Democratic Party (SP) and SP Migrants Switzerland for many years. His commitment to public service is further demonstrated by his candidacies in both the Cantonal and City Council elections in Solothurn and Olten, Switzerland, in 2017 and 2021.

He is President of The RISE Switzerland, The RISE Biggest and Most impactful GLOBAL network of Tamil Entrepreneurs and professional

Sri is fluent in German, English, and his native Tamil, a reflection of his global perspective and ability to connect with diverse communities.

Dr. Sri Rasamanickam's story is one of unwavering dedication to excellence, both in business and in service to society. His leadership continues to inspire those around him as he builds bridges across industries and cultures, leaving a lasting impact on the global stage.

Rasamanickam credits his success to his strong network and close relationships with Swiss officials and influential individuals. He joined the SP Party, which supports immigrants, and has served the immigrant community in Switzerland selflessly. This dedication earned him the position of Vice President of the SP Party's Immigration Division.

With his strong ties to one of Switzerland's leading political parties, Rasamanickam is pursuing his political ambitions. He is running for City Councilors in the upcoming election, and polls suggest a landslide victory.

This self-made businessman plans to grow his enterprises by integrating artificial intelligence into operations, ensuring customers have a delightful experience every time they ship or receive goods through Aero Lines.

He is happily married to Vasantharani, with whom he has two

children. His wife is also a partner in his business, helping him run them smoothly. When not in the boardroom, he enjoys long drives and reading books.

Business Excellence

Sri Rasamanickam's rise in the business world has been steady and systematic, achieved through commitment, hard work, and smart application of his logistics knowledge. He translated his hands-on industry experience into success for his business empire. His story is particularly inspiring, as he took a significant risk without much capital or support. His self-belief and calculated risks have paid off.

After completing his course in Logistics Management, Rasamanickam joined a logistics company, where he handled freight forwarding for various customers. He was soon promoted to Airport Manager, excelling despite his limited German skills. When his employer announced plans to close the company, Rasamanickam confidently offered to take over the business. Though his employer was skeptical, Rasamanickam's determination led him to purchase the company with borrowed funds from friends and relatives.

Aero Lines GmbH – The First Leap

In 2004, Sri Rasamanickam made a bold move when he became the owner of Aero Lines GmbH. His initial days as a business owner were filled with financial hurdles. With 10 employees relying on him and limited capital, the pressure was immense. However, with the support of his financial manager, who believed in his vision, Rasamanickam secured loans and made sound financial decisions that laid the foundation for his company. The uncertainty of that period was daunting, but he persevered with grit and determination.

In those early years, Rasamanickam displayed the instincts of a true entrepreneur, identifying market demands and seizing every opportunity that came his way. He established structured processes with checkpoints at every stage, ensuring smooth operations and consistent customer satisfaction. His foresight and meticulous planning allowed Aero Lines to grow steadily, despite the odds stacked against him.

Starting from a modest 200 sq. ft. office, Aero Lines has now expanded its footprint with fully operational offices in Switzerland, India, Sri Lanka, and Canada. The company has a vast network of associates and partners in over 150 countries, handling consignments daily. Under Rasamanickam's leadership, Aero Lines operates in a fully computerized environment, ensuring accuracy, tracking, and speed in logistics, making it a prominent player in the global market.

Aero Safe GmbH – A Vision for Security

In 2020, Rasamanickam's entrepreneurial journey took another leap when he founded Aero Safe GmbH. His strong connections with high-net-worth individuals and royal families in Switzerland revealed a critical need: secure storage for their most valuable assets. Rasamanickam recognized the importance of providing safety and security for such clientele, and thus, Aero Safe was born.

Since its inception, Aero Safe has grown steadily, offering secure storage solutions that provide peace of mind to its exclusive clientele. This venture not only stabilized Rasamanickam's business portfolio but also reaffirmed his ability to identify and meet niche market needs. His unwavering commitment to quality and security has made Aero Safe a trusted name among those seeking top-tier protection for their valuables.

Aero Courier – Expanding into New Territories

In 2015, Rasamanickam ventured into yet another industry with the founding of Aero Courier, a public limited company in Switzerland. Catering to the fast-evolving e-commerce market, Aero Courier provides both domestic and international courier services, offering efficient door-to-door delivery solutions.

With operations spanning across Switzerland, Canada, England, Sri Lanka, and India, Aero Courier quickly became a key player in the logistics and e-commerce sectors. Rasamanickam's vision for Aero Courier was simple: meet the growing demands of a rapidly digitizing world by providing reliable and fast parcel services. His deep understanding of market needs and dedication to operational excellence has positioned Aero Courier as a trusted service for both businesses and individuals.

A People-Centric Leader

One of the defining aspects of Rasamanickam's leadership is his commitment to his employees. He understands that a diverse and motivated team is the backbone of any successful business. His employees come from a range of cultural backgrounds, including India, France, Germany, Switzerland, Sri Lanka, and the USA, and Rasamanickam maintains a close, friendly relationship with each of them.

When hiring, he looks beyond formal qualifications, focusing instead on key attributes:

Multicultural adaptability: The ability to work seamlessly with individuals from diverse backgrounds.
    Attitude: A positive outlook and commitment to delivering exceptional customer service.

For Rasamanickam, these qualities are far more important than degrees or titles. He believes that a strong work ethic, cultural understanding, and a customer-first approach are what drive success in the real world.

Achievements and Acclaim

Under Rasamanickam's leadership, Aero Lines has achieved remarkable milestones:

Second-largest company at Zurich Airport for handling perishable goods, despite stiff competition from global and domestic players.

Numerous awards for excellence in the freight forwarding industry, recognizing the company's commitment to quality and reliability.

Customer satisfaction leader in Switzerland, a testament to the company's customer-first philosophy.

Words of Wisdom for Aspiring Entrepreneurs

Rasamanickam's journey from employee to successful business owner is a source of inspiration for aspiring entrepreneurs. His advice is simple yet profound:

Build strong networks: Success is often about who you know and the relationships you cultivate.

Never stop learning: Stay curious and adaptable. The business world is ever-changing, and those who thrive are always evolving.

Stay ahead of industry trends: Attend exhibitions, workshops, and events to stay informed on the latest market demands and innovations.

Customer focus is key: Prioritize your customers and always maintain the right attitude, no matter the challenges you face.

Awards and Accolades

Rasamanickam was the first person from Sri Lanka to apply for Swiss citizenship and received a warm welcome from the Swiss City government in Olten. He is the first Sri Lankan to achieve permanent Swiss citizenship. His accolades include:

- **Member of the Year Award (2012, 2013, 2015, 2017):** Awarded by WWPC Network, a USA-based global logistics network, in recognition of Aero Lines GmbH's outstanding performance as a member.
- **Vice President of the Immigrants Division Solothurn, SP Party, Switzerland:** Recognized for his selfless support to the immigrant community, the SP Party appointed Rasamanickam as Vice President of its Immigrant Wing, boosting his reputation among both immigrants and local citizens.
- **Future City Councilors:** With polls favoring his victory in the upcoming election, Rasamanickam's political career looks promising.
- He is President of The RISE Switzerland, The RISE Biggest and Most impactful GLOBAL network of Tamil Entrepreneurs and professional

Conclusion

What sets Sri Rasamanickam apart is his ability to turn adversity into opportunity. Fleeing his home country due to civil war, he sought refuge in Switzerland, where he worked his way up from humble beginnings to build a business empire. His success in the highly competitive Swiss market serves as a testament to his perseverance, hard work, and strategic thinking.

Today, Sri Rasamanickam manages three successful companies

and plans to start a fourth, showing that his entrepreneurial journey is far from over. As he embarks on a political career, his story offers inspiration not only to aspiring entrepreneurs but also to anyone facing challenges in life. His belief in continuous learning, strong networking, and maintaining a customer-focused approach has led him to where he is today, proving that success is possible even in the face of great adversity.

Dr. Sri Rasamanickam

Dr. Sri Rasamanickam
A Visionary Entrepreneur in Logistics and Supply Chain Management

Dr. Sri Rasamanickam is an **entrepreneur**, a **global leader** in **logistics** and **supply chain management** with over **25 years** of experience in steering multinational organizations to success. As the **Founder** and **CEO** of **Aero Lines GmbH** in **Zurich, Switzerland**, he has overseen the **strategic growth** of the company, establishing it as a prominent **freight forwarder** and **logistics service provider** across Europe and beyond.

Dr. Rasamanickam's expertise spans **operational management**, **performance optimization**, and **financial strategy**, which have resulted in **sustainable growth** and **profitability** for his ventures. His entrepreneurial spirit has led him to find several successful enterprises, including **Aero Safe GmbH**, specializing in **security** and **asset protection**, and **Aero Courier**, offering **e-commerce** and **parcel services** in multiple countries.

His distinguished career is further complemented by prestigious **certifications** from global aviation authorities and academic achievements, such as a **European Professional Doctorate** from **Rushford Business School** in **Geneva, Switzerland**. Dr. Rasamanickam is also actively involved in **politics**, serving as a member of the **Election Commission** in **Olten, Switzerland**, and advocating for **social democratic policies** as part of various political organizations.

Fluent in **German, English,** and **Tamil**, Dr. Rasamanickam is a recognized **thought leader** and **innovator** in the logistics sector, dedicated to building strong **global partnerships** and mentoring future leaders in the industry.

Reach out to Dr. Sri: linkedin.com/in/srirasamanickam

Let's Connect

Email sgninfo@signaturegln.com requesting to join Kristy Guo's Signature Growth Academy to empower world leaders and if you want to be the next International Best-seller author and get Kristy to be your coach for your life and business.

Follow Kristy Guo
LinkedIn – Cuilan (Kristy) Guo
www.linkedin.com/in/cuilan-kristy-guo-1776b5182
Facebook – Kristy Guo
https://www.facebook.com/kristy.guo.3/
https://www.facebook.com/kristyguochangemaker/
YouTube: The Joyful Leader In You
https://youtube.com/@TheJoyfulLeaderInYou-ot6qk

Special Thanks to

Eastrong International Logistics Co., Ltd.
Eastrong (eastrongintl.com)

Stephen Feng
President

Eric Chen
Global Network Director

Powered by

The Logistics Legends

Connect with Kristy by scanning the code above

Connect with SGN by scanning the code above

Resources

Approximately **2.6 million people** are employed in the logistics industry in the UK, according to recent estimates. This includes roles in transport, warehousing, freight forwarding, supply chain management, and related areas. The logistics sector represents around **8% of the UK workforce**, highlighting its importance in supporting the country's economy and supply chains.

In the UK, around 2.5 million people work in the logistics industry, contributing significantly to sectors like transportation, warehousing, and supply chain management. This represents roughly 3.75% of the total UK population, which is about 67 million. Logistics plays a key role in supporting various industries, from retail to manufacturing, driving both local and international trade(

Logistics UK

Logistics UK

If approximately 2.5 million people work in logistics out of a total UK population of 67 million, this means that roughly 1 in every 27 people in the UK works in the logistics industry.

Here's how it breaks down:

- Total UK population: 67 million
- People working in logistics: 2.5 million

Calculation:
67,000,000 ÷ 2,500,000 = 26.8, or about 1 in 27 people work in logistics.

Why is logistics people's impact significant?

- **Global Trade Enabler:**
    - Logistics is vital for global trade. In the U.S. alone, the logistics industry accounts for nearly **8% of the GDP**, supporting trillions of dollars of goods moving through the supply chain. According to the Council of Supply Chain Management Professionals (CSCMP), U.S. logistics costs reached **$1.6 trillion in 2022**, representing the industry's sheer scale and economic importance.

- **Employment Impact:**
    - In the U.S., logistics employs millions of people across various roles, such as supply chain management, warehousing, and transportation. In 2022, **4.7 million people** were directly involved in transportation and material moving roles, highlighting how crucial this workforce is to the movement of goods. Source: Bureau of Labor Statistics (BLS).

- **Growth and Job Creation:**
    - As e-commerce expands, demand for logistics and warehousing has surged. Projections indicate that **logisticians' roles are expected to grow by 28%** from 2021 to 2031 in the U.S., far outpacing average job growth rates. This signals increasing reliance on logistics professionals to meet the needs of modern commerce. Source: U.S. BLS.

- **Efficiency and Cost Control:**
  - Efficient logistics systems can significantly reduce operational costs for businesses. The use of advanced logistics and supply chain practices saves companies on average **10-20% in operational costs**, boosting profitability across sectors. Source: CSCMP.

- **Environmental Impact:**
  - Logistics workers are also central to reducing environmental impact. Green supply chain initiatives aim to reduce carbon footprints, with some estimates showing that optimizing logistics can cut emissions by **up to 15%** in some sectors. Source: World Economic Forum.

"Time for you to be the next logistics legend!"

Kristy Guo

www.ingramcontent.com/pod-product-compliance
Lightning Source LLC
Chambersburg PA
CBHW071957290426
44109CB00018B/2057